CULTURES IN DIALOGUE

Series Editors: Teresa Heffernan and Reina Lewis

SERIES ONE

ORIENTALISM, OCCIDENTALISM, AND WOMEN'S WRITING

CULTURES IN DIALOGUE

SERIES ONE

Volume 11

AN ENGLISHWOMAN IN
A TURKISH HAREM

THE AUTHOR IN TURKISH COSTUME

AN ENGLISHWOMAN IN
A TURKISH HAREM

BY

GRACE ELLISON

WITH AN INTRODUCTION BY
EDWARD G. BROWNE, M.A., F.B.A., F.R.C.P.

New Introduction by
Teresa Heffernan and Reina Lewis

GORGIAS PRESS
2007

First Gorgias Press Edition, 2007.

Copyright © 2007 by Gorgias Press LLC.

ISBN 978-1-59333-211-2

GORGIAS PRESS
46 Orris Ave., Piscataway, NJ 08854 USA
www.gorgiaspress.com

CULTURES IN DIALOGUE

Series Editors: Teresa Heffernan and Reina Lewis

Cultures in Dialogue returns to active circulation out of print sources by women writers from the East and the West. Tracing cross-cultural and intra-cultural exchanges over three centuries, this project brings to light women's engagement with discourses of gender emancipation, imperialism, nationalism, Islam, and modernity. While the figure of Woman—Orientalized and Occidentalized—has been a central and fought over symbol in the construction of an East/West divide, women's own texts have been marginalized. Focusing on dialogue instead of divide, *Cultures in Dialogue* uses women's varied and contestatory contributions to reconsider the historical tensions between Eastern and Western cultures, offering a nuanced understanding of their current manifestations.

SERIES ONE:

ORIENTALISM, OCCIDENTALISM, AND WOMEN'S WRITING

Series One of *Cultures in Dialogue*, consisting of a mix of memoir, travelogue, ethnography, and political commentary, considers the exchanges between and amongst Ottoman and British and American women from the 1880s up to the 1940s. The seismic shift in the understanding of identity as the Ottoman Empire was rapidly being displaced at the end of the nineteenth-century opened up a space for discussions about female liberty and its relationship to Islamic, Turkish, and Western nationalism, about the gendering of private and public spheres, about rural/urban tensions and questions of class mobility, about the status of the harem, and about colonial and imperial interests. In the nineteenth-century the cosmopolitan Islamic Ottoman Empire began to shift from a concept of citizenship based on belief to one based on place of birth, culminating in an independent Turkey and radically altering the relationship of women to the nation. In this complicated exchange, some elite Ottoman women, who refused Orientalist portrayals of themselves as enslaved, asserted an agency and nostalgically invested in this disappearing culture whilst others rejected the old ways in favor of modernizing the nation. So too, some Western women, enjoying the status and luxuries Ottoman culture afforded, replicated even as they challenged Orientalist tropes. Further there were Western women promoting the force of empire, in the name of civilization. Where some bound feminism to imperialism and modernity, other Eastern and Western women interrupted this collusion, opening up other avenues and other models of feminism.

The twelve volumes in Series One trace the range of opinion found among Western and Ottoman women in this period, offering a chance to see how their dialogue influenced and defined each others' views. They also illustrate the challenges of writing about Ottoman female life when the harem featured both as a desirable cultural commodity in Western harem literature and as the socializing spatial relations that both facilitated discussions of female emancipation and were the subject of debate in the Islamic and Western world.

For some women, the release from veiling and seclusion promised personal and political liberty, crucial to the reform of the imperial sultanic regime. Other women viewed the shift to the modern nation with more ambivalence, understanding it as a surrendering of a long-standing agency available to elite Ottoman women. The British author Grace Ellison, for instance, was a reluctant suffragist whose repeated visits to Turkey convinced her that the luxury and protection enjoyed by elite Ottoman women should not be too quickly abandoned for Western models of female independence. Zeyneb Hanoum, on the other hand, was a Muslim Ottoman who initially longed to escape from the restrictions of the harem, dreaming of Western freedom and actively resisting the racialized portrayals of Ottoman women as passive odalisques. However she was sorely disappointed when, during her travels in Europe, she came to understand Western women as differently but as equally confined. Both writers explored the double-edged sword of modernity as they nostalgically invested in an already vanishing model of Ottoman femininity. Veiling, following the tradition of Lady Mary Wortley Montagu in the eighteenth century, was sometimes read by Western writers subversively as permitting sexual agency and also, as was the case with Ellison, as offering the possibility of passing as "other." So too, for Eastern women veiling and seclusion were not necessarily about lack of power; rather, for elite women, such as Melek Hanoum, within the different Ottoman conceptualization of the public, the segregated household guaranteed their access to power.

Unlike Ellison, however, there were Western women who traveled to the Orient with a less complicated and more typically Orientalist and colonialist mission of "liberating" Turkish women from their slavery. Lady Annie Brassey, for example, was opposed to women getting the vote in England, which renders suspect her desire to "free" the veiled woman and exposes her imperialist interests. Privileged Ottoman women, nevertheless, as suggested in the accounts of women such as Musbah Haidar, enjoyed as much freedom to travel and were as educated as Western women like Brassey, further challenging Western stereotypes. Yet there were also Ottoman women, such as Halide Adivar Edib, who rejected the nostalgic investment in Ottoman identity in favor of a Turkish nationalist discourse of progress and modernization. This shift toward nationalism, however, threatened the cosmopolitan nature of Ottoman society. The new model provoked writers like Demetra Vaka Brown, a Greek Christian who was able to claim allegiance to an Ottoman Empire but who was necessarily excluded from a Turkish nation, to protest the imposition of national boundaries even as writers like Lucy Garnett promoted, in her obsessive attempt to categorize the women of Turkey, a racialized understanding of nationalism. But not all Western writers were as oblivious to the impact of the increasingly segregated Empire. Anna Bowman Dodd protested the presence of American missionaries who actively fermented dissent amongst Armenian Christians by teaching them they were "better" than Muslims. Selma Ekrem, from a renowned and progressive Muslim family, also discussed the negative impact of the model of racialized nationalism on what had been an inclusive and multi-ethnic empire.

If understandings of the nation, of private and public spaces, and of liberty differed across the East/West divide, so too did the understanding of class. The Ottoman system was not based primarily on lineage and blood and allowed for considerable social mobility, as was the case with Melek Hanoum, who married into the Muslim bureaucratic elite from relatively humble Greek/Armenian Christian origins. Given that literacy and foreign languages were for most of this period the preserve of the educated elite, it is no surprise that all the Eastern writers in this series came from this predominantly urban sector, many of them hailing from prominent families. Despite the social positions of the authors, still, traces of non-elite women's lives feature as integral to the social relations witnessed in Ottoman women's accounts. The investigations of Western writers, such as Hester Donaldson Jenkins, also touch specifically on the lives of subaltern women. Although these authors focus on cosmopolitan centers, such as Istanbul, provincial and rural life is also covered, particularly in the work of the American author Ruth Frances Woodsmall, who like many traveled widely in the region.

Feminist Dialogues Across Cultures: An English Woman in a Turkish Harem and the Turkish Harem in an English Woman

Teresa Heffernan and Reina Lewis

REFLECTIONS ON AUTHORSHIP AND HAREM LITERATURE

On opening the double page spread for the title page of this book, the reader is faced with several pieces of evocative information that locate this book and its author as part of an international web of writers and experts. The book appears with an introduction by Edward Granville Browne (1862–1926), the renowned Cambridge scholar. Before the reader even gets to the contents of his introduction, the presence of his name on the front page endorses Ellison's work, bringing to bear the full weight of his expertise in Persian and Ottoman literature, his reputation as a traveller, and his professional associations as a member of the British Academy. But Grace Ellison's own professional status is also signalled with promotional

We would like to thank St. Mary's University, Halifax, and the School of Social Sciences, Media, and Cultural Studies, University of East London, for their financial support.

v*

information on the facing page about her two other publications in this field. "By the same author" gives us two other books, produced "in collaboration with" Melek Hanoum and Zeyneb Hanoum. The names of her collaborators would have been recognisably "Oriental" or Ottoman to her contemporaries, and the titles of their books *Abdul Hamid's Daughter*, referring to the late Ottoman sultan, and *A Turkish Woman's European Impressions*, emphasised the Ottoman or Turkish nature of the books' material. All of this serves to immerse Grace Ellison in a network of international connections not just as a traveller—the basis for her experiences in a "Turkish Harem"—but as a professional writer and editor. If she does not have letters of professional validation after her name, her status and expertise is endorsed by this evidence of her activities as collaborator with Ottoman writers.

That Ellison's book needs at once to establish her authority in the field is not simply a standard publisher's marketing ploy: in harem literature, her chosen area of endeavour, conventions of authorial integrity were key to the validation of the work. Emerging during the nineteenth century as a subgenre of the broader field of travel writing, harem literature is a type of writing that especially privileges women writers who had access to a space that was closed to Western men. Accounts of harem life, as seen in this series, were therefore a realm of reportage that was widely acknowledged to be female territory. With the West endlessly curious about the much fantasised goings on in Eastern harems, Western women set out to supply information, sometimes challenging Western Orientalist stereotypes, sometimes repeating them, often writing with a mixture of both. By the time that Ellison published this book, in the early months of the First World War in 1915, opportunities for women to visit the Middle East had increased dramatically due to advances in travel technology and to developments in Western women's social status that made travel, with male relatives and, increasingly, unaccompanied, a more common experience. But although more women were travelling to the region, and writing about their experiences, Ellison is unusual as someone who travelled independently for professional purposes—the material in her book, as we discover in her preface, had its genesis as reports for the British newspaper the *Daily Telegraph*.

The expedition that produced the *Daily Telegraph* articles was, in fact, Ellison's third visit to Istanbul (or Constantinople as it was known in the West at the time). Her initial acquaintance with the city came whilst she was still at school in 1905, though she managed soon thereafter to return as a cub reporter in 1908 with the enviable job of covering the inauguration of the constitutional government, after the Young Turk revolution. It was on this assignment that she met Kâmil Paşa (1832–1913), then grand vizier to Sultan Abdülhamit II, and befriended his daughter Makboulè Hanim—the woman, referred to as "Fâtima" who was to be her hostess during her protracted visit in the autumn/winter of 1913–14. Her reports to the *Daily Telegraph*, titled "Life in the Harem," appeared almost daily in January and February 1914, in the anxious months leading up to the First World War. By the time these writings were extended into book form, the war had started, and Ellison ends her volume with notes from the hospital in France where she was serving as a nurse. As is evident from *An Englishwoman in a Turkish Harem*, Ellison moved in elevated political circles in Istanbul, and achieved in Europe a position of considerable professional status, yet frustratingly little is known about the details of her life.

Ellison was born in Scotland (date unknown), and educated in England, attending Rochester Girl's grammar school, and in France, where she went on to university in Halle. This dual educational experience would have provided her with the fluency in French that was to be such an asset in Turkey, where French was the non-Oriental language most commonly spoken by educated Ottomans. Ellison started her journalistic career as continental (European) correspondent for the *Bystander*, pursuing a concern with international affairs in 1907 with a commission to report on the Hague Conference on international armament control for the *Daily Graphic*. As well as writing, Ellison was involved in nursing and was one of the founders of the French Female Nursing Corps, where she served as Directice Générale, undertaking a nine month fundraising tour of the United States to establish the Florence Nightingale Hospital in Bordeaux. Her association with international nursing continued at the end of the First World War, when in 1918, she took the position of assistant to the head of the American Red Cross children's welfare bureaux. Her services in France were recognised with awards such as the medialle d'or d'honneur, and the silver medal of the French foreign office. Her death in 1935 was marked with an obituary in *The Times* (October 4, 1935), which recorded her nursing work as well as her many publications, but gives little information about the rest of her life. Ellison, who never married (and there is no record of any romantic attachments), came from a moderately well-off family, and, though she may have had some independent income, was certainly sympathetic to the difficulties faced by women in Britain who found it hard to earn a respectable living. Though evidently fond of her own brother, she bristled about the inequities faced by women reliant on brotherly largess in her tract on British feminist politics, *The Disadvantages of Being a Woman* (1922). She was likely not dependent herself and relied on the money generated by her writing and other professional roles. Her condemnation of "pin-money women," whose dilettante literary dabbling deprived honest women writers of a living wage, makes clear that she took her own writing, and its financial rewards, seriously (Ellison 1923: 73).

Inspired by the travel tales of her military father, Captain Ellison, Grace went on to follow *An Englishwoman in a Turkish Harem* with a series of books derived from her European war-time experiences and subsequent journeys to Turkey, Syria, Palestine, and the Balkans. Building on the evident success of the first book, Ellison published similarly branded volumes such as *An Englishwoman in the French Firing Line* (1915), *An Englishwoman in Occupied Germany* (1920, both publishers unknown), and finally, *An Englishwoman in Angora* (Hutchinson, 1923). This last, along with *Turkey To-day* (Hutchinson, 1923), often refers back to her earlier experiences in the region and to the lasting friendships she had forged. In this, Ellison was exceptional, not only for the longevity of her alliances with Ottoman women, but for the extent to which these connections were overtly political in their focus and part of a shared literary professional exchange between Western and Eastern women.

Ellison fosters a dialogue between Western and Ottoman women that she documented in her writing and perpetuated through her editorial work: she frequently quotes leading

Ottoman feminists and reformers such as Halide Edib; devotes a chapter to publicising the work of Turkish women poets and writers; and, most significantly, worked to bring into print the writings of her friends, the sisters known as Zeyneb Hanoum and Melek Hanoum. Famous as the Ottoman Muslim women whose clandestine correspondence and meetings with the French author Pierre Loti had informed his hugely successful novel *Les Désenchantées*, the two women had fled to France just before its publication in 1906. Meeting Ellison there, the three women began a correspondence and a professional association that was to last for years. As part of her mission to promote the cause of Turkey to a suspicious Europe, and to further the emancipation of Turkish women in particular, Ellison edited one book by each sister, also providing an introduction to each based on her experiences in Turkey. As well as flagging these collaborative publications at the start of *An Englishwoman in a Turkish Harem*, Ellison's first single-authored book repeatedly references her connection to the sisters, and through them to Loti (out of fashion now, but famous then as the purveyor of popular Orientalist romances), marking her book as an intervention into the field of harem literature. Yet this was no straightforward literary genre: as for the Ottoman sisters, and other writers in this series, the market for Ellison's writing relied on Western Orientalist curiosity about the evocative space of the segregated Muslim household, making it almost impossible to avoid the very stereotypes that some women authors wanted to challenge. This was the double bind of harem literature, and Ellison's book starts out with a title full of evocative terms that she knew would help sales. Classifications like "Englishwoman" and "Turkish harem" do not simply indicate geographical locations: the fruitful contrast of gender, religions, and nationality keyed into a set of knowledges about the presumed differences between East and West, and Christianity and Islam, whose imagined incompatibility Ellison set out to disprove.

She is quite explicit about the demands of the market, informing the reader by page fifteen that a "chapter, at least, on harem life will always add to the value of the book," many of which "are written, not to extend the truth about a people, but only to sell." This prurient interest, she immediately points out, was because of the predictable Western fantasies of countless available and delectable women subject to the power of the "polygamous master." Although her next sentences shatter the fantasy—"the Turk loves his home and he loves his wife. He is an indulgent husband and kind father" (15)—a look at her own table of contents reveals a list of topics that might well play up to the expectations of the Western reader. This need to produce a cultural commodity that could function within the remit of harem literature whilst also challenging Western misapprehensions is the tension that drives Ellison's book. In this context, it is the contemporaneity of her experiences and the specificity of her connections that give value to her account and that anchor her observations, allowing her to operate within harem literature and reportage at the same time as she provides evidence contrary to Western fantasies. In this light, the book's dedication to "all those who made my visit so interesting," as well as its title, emphasises the being-there-ness of Ellison's account. Yet, she must meet as well as confound reader expectations, and by the end of chapter three she has managed to include nearly all of the themes typical of harem literature, with references to harem life, polygamy, slavery, the veil, female education, religion, "primitive people," and descriptions of Istanbul. Ellison, however, puts a new spin on these stereotypical topics, often emphasising the modernisation of Ottoman life. One of the ways Ellison negotiates this tension is by mixing accounts of the ideas and habits of older generations of women (for whose attractive "traditional" raiment and gracious habits she is already nostalgic) with a contrasting picture of the desires and behaviours of the modernising progressive Ottoman elite with whom she was connected in Istanbul.

It is not just prominent women that she meets: her book is full of conversations and meetings with diplomats and military men, and luminaries of the Young Turk Committee of Union and Progress (CUP) such as Enver Paşa and Cemal (Djémal) Paşa, as well as her connection to "Fâtima's" illustrious father. One needs also to recognise that not all the major figures in the book are identified by name: because of concern about the political repercussions of talking to foreigners in a period marked by revolution, counter-revolution, and war, Ellison did not identify the people she had personal relationships with until later publications. So in this early book, Fâtima's father, Kâmil Paşa, has no name and neither does his daughter; nor does she identify Fâtima's husband, Nagdi Bey, also a public figure who served in the (increasingly pro-German) government of Enver Paşa that had replaced the pro-British cabinet of Kâmil Paşa. This need for discretion may explain why Kâmil Paşa's death is reported by Ellison with the euphemism that he was "spending the winter in Cyprus," when in fact he had been exiled there by the CUP government after his role in the failed anti-CUP countercoup of March 1913. Ellison does, in her introduction to Melek Hanoum's *Abdul Hamid's Daughter*, draw on her experience of meeting the book's heroine, Princess Aiche, to whom she was introduced by Makboulé Hanim, but again the name of this contact is suppressed.

Yet, despite all her elevated connections, despite having been published in a quality newspaper, despite having already brought into print two related books, Grace Ellison still introduces this book with a preface whose self-depreciations belie the seriousness of her professional and literary ambitions. Denigrating her writing as "only" an Englishwoman's "'impressions" of harem life, and contending that her "letters" do not "claim to be a psychological study of Turkish character" or a "political or historical treatise," she then proceeds to explain that her aim is to "correct" the "errors, prejudice, and hatred which have become almost part of the British national 'attitude' towards Turkey" (vii). This, indeed, is the stuff of politics, of history, and of psychology: to alter attitudes in these arenas, even in "ever so small a way" is hardly a mean ambition.

BRITISH-TURKISH RELATIONS

Grace Ellison's desire to write a book that would serve as a corrective to English prejudice towards Turks, the people she had come to embrace, was expressed at a moment of massive historical change in Ottoman/European relations. Visiting Turkey in the year leading up to the First World War and revising her *Telegraph* reports for publication as it started, Ellison was in a position to observe many of the events that were to lead to the eventual establishment of the modern Turkish state. By the time she was writing her afterward to this volume in 1915, the Ottoman Empire had entered the Great War on the side of

Germany, and for this was to be punished by the victorious Allies, especially Britain, whose five year occupation of Istanbul (1918–1924) was part of an aggressively imperialist project to carve up the Ottoman Empire into a series of successor states over whom the Western powers intended to exert influence. The once mighty Empire did collapse, but the nationalists fought hard to salvage the Republic of Turkey from its ruin, and, under the leadership of Mustapha Kemal Paşa, abandoned the international project of the Empire for a fiercely nationalist stance, moving the capital from the cosmopolitan heart of the Empire to the scarcely populated Ankara. However, even prior to the War, various versions of national consciousness were already circulating as the Young Turks had successfully revolted against the absolutism of Sultan Abdülhamit II in 1908, liberating the Empire from thirty years of despotic rule and restoring the constitution of 1876. Ellison is writing from this liminal place in history as the Empire is trying to negotiate the impossible divide between the diversity of its population and a racialized version of the modern nation. This irreconcilable tension accounts for some of the odd silences in her narrative: her embrace of "Turks" was limited to a particular segment of the Ottoman population and she has little to say on other minorities and religions inhabiting the Empire. Even as the Islamic Ottoman press of the day was critical of the term the "Turkish government"—Ellison favours it over Ottoman and uses the term Turk as a religious but even more so an ethnic category, suggesting her implicit support for a national rather than a multinational consciousness.

Through much of the nineteenth century Britain had for strategic reasons supported and defended this declining Eastern Empire in order to ensure, amongst other things, that its overland route to India was secure and to nurture economic interests in Turkey, which was a healthy market for British exports. Much as it did with its colonies, Britain had mined Turkey for its raw material and then sold her back manufactured goods made with them. But Britain, since its occupation of Egypt in 1882, was no longer as preoccupied with defending its Indian route, and its own growing confidence in its strength as a colonial power made it less dependent on the economically depressed Ottoman Empire that, impoverished by its wars with

Greece, Russia, and the Balkans, could no longer afford its lavish and extravagant spending on foreign manufactured goods. If one of the reasons polygamy had become rare in twentieth-century Turkey was, as Ellison discusses, because the well-educated Turkish man was now mortified by the very thought of having a harem of dependent women instead of an equally educated partner at his side as a mark of his modernity and that the modern Turkish woman would no longer "tolerate a rival in her own home," the other had to do with cost. "'When four wives meant to their possessor four tillers of the land,' said a witty Pasha, the other day, 'there was some sense in polygamy, but not now when they buy their dresses at Paquin's'" (57). Straitened finances applied not only to the affluent elite, among whom polygamy had been more common than in the rest of the population, but also to the imperial family itself. Ellison documents the passing of a decree forbidding polygamy in the Imperial household: "the Young Turkey can no longer afford to keep these ever-recurring princes" (126). Ellison also criticizes European exploitation of Turkish resources and markets which had contributed to the country's debt and argues that Turkey should never have trusted Europe for help: "The duty of Europe should have been to help the Turks to help themselves, instead of which all along the line they have stepped in and taken the bread from their mouths" (62).

But if Britain, at the height of its own power, was no longer as keenly interested in the bankrupt Ottoman Empire, the other countries surrounding her continued to exert a great influence. Russia still had ambitions in Turkey; Germany, since the 1880s, had been courting the Empire and training its troops, replacing France and Britain as the military supporter of the Ottoman; and France still held its own as the intellectual center and breeding ground for the revolutionary Young Turks in exile. Ellison's close friendship with Turks and keen interest in the country is framed by her larger interest in wanting to rekindle and foster the relationship between the Turks and the English. Encouraging England to think of itself as the moral guide of this nation in the making and to help her in her struggle for liberty and modernization, Ellison writes that for the Turks: "England stands for all that is good and honest and just. England is the fairy godmother, who, with a touch of her magic wand, could put everything straight for them" (152). Reminding her audience that Britain had come to Turkey's defense in the Crimean War (1854–6), Ellison refers several times to the immense gratitude Turks feel for Britain, given the blood its men shed for her (in actual fact, France, who also came to Turkey's defense, had lost many more men). By the time of her afterword, nursing casualties in France, Ellison writes of the consequence of British neglect and abandonment of Turkey, as Germany, having successfully wooed Turkey with money and military support, had succeeded in gaining her allegiance in the Great War.

For the most part Britain had come to the defense of the Ottoman Empire, with the notable exception of British support for the War of Greek independence (1821–32). But, as Ellison was writing, England was ready to step away and entertain the disintegration of this vast territory. Nevertheless England's legacy and influence had affected the course of events in Turkey and laid the groundwork for its transformation from a multi-ethnic and cosmopolitan Empire to a modern nation founded on a shared ethnic and racial identity. The once celebrated inter-racial mixing of the Empire, where, for instance, the royal consorts selected by the first two generations of Ottomans were neither Muslim nor Turkish, was now, in a climate of increasing racial antagonism and as modern Turkey started to take shape, implicitly condemned. Nineteenth-century British and American travel literature to the Ottoman Empire reflects the anxiety this miscegenation provoked as it foreclosed the idea of a dominant race, which was critical to the racialized understanding of the nation in the West. See, for instance, Anna Bowman Dodd in this series, who comments about Istanbul that the "streets through which we were presently swept were filled with as strange and wonderful a world of men. The faces of these men were the faces of brown men, of white men, of black men. No two faces seemed to belong to the same race; and no one garb or costume appeared to have been the model chosen for repetition" (6). As the home of the embassies and minority populations, Pera had for centuries been one of the most cosmopolitan areas of the city. As the social, economic and diplomatic center, its inhabitants had always been viewed with some suspicion, often referred to as pirates and scoundrels. However by the time Ellison is writing, they are viewed suspiciously in part because the racial mixing facilitated by the diversity of the place challenges a clear national identification; she reports that a Turkish woman dismisses Perotes because they have "the blood of six nations in their veins and the soul of none" (14).

The nineteenth-century Tanzimat reforms (1839–1876) that restructured the Ottoman Empire were heavily influenced by French revolutionary ideals and British foreign policy, and the foundations for them were laid earlier in the century under the guidance of Straford Canning, the British Ambassador at Constantinople, who served off and on from 1825 to 1858. These Westernizing reforms that culminated in the Constitution and parliament of 1876 paved the way for the emergence of modern Turkey after the collapse of the Empire. On the one hand, these reforms, in theory, guaranteed the equality of Muslim and non-Muslim citizens before the law; introduced secular schools, and standardized taxation. On the other hand, they promoted the centralization of the state, decreased the autonomy of the provinces, and encouraged a homogenous ethnic and racial identification. By the middle of the nineteenth century, the term "Turkish," which had long been used by the British to refer to Ottomans and which generally meant Muslim, was now sometimes being used in the local newspapers to suggest a racial and ethnic identification—an indication of both Western influence on the Empire and on the growing nationalist movements within it. This shift was also evident in the changes in the semi-autonomous *millet* system, the inter-communal and inter-racial administrative units that had long been organized along religious lines and whose borders were in constant flux. Under the Tanzimat reforms, however, increasingly *millets* came to be understood as nations in the modern sense.

It was in the midst of European incursions in the Empire and national liberation movements amongst the Greeks, Arabs, Macedonians, and Armenians (that led to the Balkan war and fueled the Great War) that the Young Turks emerged. In 1908, the Committee of Union and Progress seized power from the autocratic Sultan Abdülhamit II, who had turned his back on the West and was in turn vilified by it. Under his controversial reign, he had both abolished the constitution and attempted to preserve the diversity of his Empire and his international status as imperial ruler. His promotion of pan-Islamism aimed to extend his influence as Caliph beyond the Ottoman territories, reaching out to Muslims in India and elsewhere as a counter to Western nationalism and imperialism. While in the early days of the twentieth century, most Muslims, in Istanbul at least, remained dedicated to their Osmanlı roots and remained anti-nationalist in the modern sense, a small group of the elite Young Turks supported the homogenizing of the nation along ethnic and racial lines, turning against Turkey's multi-racial heritage that had found its last real expression under the penultimate Sultan. Organizations such as the Turkish Hearth, which had started up in Istanbul in 1912, restricted attendance to Turkish Muslims, refusing to admit other nationalities, and promoted the study of the Turkish race and culture. The feminist meeting that Ellison attends in chapter six operates along these nationalist lines and Ellison largely ignores other factions of the Young Turk revolutionaries who were inclusive of other minorities and who entertained alternatives to nationalism, such as socialism. Ellison had also arrived in the aftermath of the Balkan war (1912–13), where the Ottoman Empire had experienced devastating losses of its territories as the combined Christian forces of Greece, Serbia, Bulgaria, and Montenegro succeeded in defeating the overly confident Turkish armies in a matter of weeks and long held Ottoman provinces broke away from the Empire and asserted their independence. Serbia, Bulgaria, and Greece fought over Macedonia and Greece greatly increased its national boundaries, winning Crete amongst other areas. The strong support of America and Britain for the Christian forces and the pressure of these losses further increased the support for Turkish nationalism, a seemingly necessary response to both Western imperialism and the independence movements threatening the Empire.

Edward Browne, in his introduction to Ellison, although in general supportive of Turkish patriots who had fought to liberate Turkey and the project of "National Awakening," is critical of aspects of the nationalizing impulse. Referring to the "vain and disastrous attempt to Turkify or Ottomanize the various non-Turkish elements of the Ottoman Empire," he raises an issue that Ellison never fully addresses in her book. In particular, the Young Turks desire to change the script from Arabic to Latin, to standardize the language of the Empire and impose Turkish on, for instance, Armenians and Albanians, to "purify" Turkish vocabulary and exile Persian and Arabic words is seen by Browne to work against what he understands as the generosity and hospitality and openness of the Turks, qualities he feels Ellison so accurately described in her book. Ignoring the history of British influence in the Empire, he attributes these negative changes to the "chauvinistic" French who have encouraged an "insular" way of thinking amongst these revolutionary Turks. Ellison herself never comes to terms with this particular aspect of the Turkish reforms. Resistance to the legacy of Western imperialism fostered the promotion of "'Turkey for the Turks," which required to some degree re-imagining the nation in terms of a mythic and exclusive coherence, a move that clashed with the legacy of hospitality and tolerance that she so admires. While the term Turkish is still very much in flux during this period, it is clear, as she scarcely mentions the other minorities of the Empire and is strangely quiet on the Armenian situation, that her agenda is both nationalist and feminist in focus. In her chapter on Turkish women writers, she presents evidence of Ottoman women's cultural agency as a direct riposte to Western presumptions of their gendered ignorance. Ellison then segues into a discussion of male writers responsible for the development of a new, and to her ideologically valuable, tradition of literature in Turkish and in so doing brings back reference to Zeyneb Hanoum and Melek Hanoum and their grandfather's connection to one of the great Ottoman authors, Şinasi, taking the opportunity once again to promote her collaboration with them. In this Ellison participates in the very nationalism that Brown is critical of in his introduction as she tries to map out an exclusively female and Turkish literature that would parallel the male canon.

RACE, NATIONALISM, AND FEMINISM

Although Ellison is fully supportive of Turkey's project to modernize, she is nevertheless nostalgic for what she understands as traditional life in the Orient, "for the passing of the primitive Turk" (164). In the opening pages, she describes the restful, timeless, tranquil East which she contrasts with the bustle, speed, and noise of the West that she complains, "deaden one's understanding." Traditionally, Orientalism coded the East negatively as feminine—as passive, exotic, and indolent. Ellison continues with this stereotype of the East as feminine but re-codes it as positive in the same way that domestic space was imagined by some in the Victorian era as a place for men to recover in and return to after their day negotiating the transient and fast-paced capitalist market place. That Ellison was aware of the discrepancy between the tranquil home and the reality of the women trapped within its confines, and between the harem as restorative and at the same time oppressive, explains the tension in her work between the nostalgia she expresses and her support of modernization. And, very clearly, Ellison's main interest in the political reforms and the emergence of the new nation are the promises they hold out to women. As she establishes early on in her narrative, whatever criticism the West heaps on the new Turkey, the opening of such things as a woman's restaurant in Istanbul, where women gather and openly discuss politics, is the hallmark of this new government and speaks to the massive progress that has been made in the area of female emancipation. But Ellison also saw in the Turkish movement the possibility of an alternate feminism, different from the version that had found expression in Europe, so she never advocates a complete turn away from the tradition, custom, and religion of the East as she sees Turkey as a country "where brotherhood and equality have been best understood." She writes: "I have not defended the harem system. There is, however, so much in the Turkish home which is beautiful that I would prefer to see them progressing on the lines of their own civilization, rather than becoming a poor imitation of us" (198). Ellison is thus sympathetic with some of the Ottoman feminists, such as Fâtima Alié Hanoum (1862–1936), who are also critical of the adoption of Western styles of dress and attitudes, preferring to retain such practices as veiling.

Thrust into the market and the competitive and individualistic world that capitalism fosters, Western women both lack protection and the communal comfortable space that Ellison is alternately drawn to and critical of in her experience of various harems, craving both solitude and privacy even as she appreciates the constant attention paid to her. On her visit to the

Imperial Harem she longs to fling aside the "lattice-work" that closes off its inhabitants from the outside world and simultaneously recognizes that they may well "turn their backs in horror on the ugly unprotected existence of some of the women of my country" (37). Pointing to the dark side of freedom, Ellison suggests that Western women, for all their liberty, lack "the blessing of protection" (196). If the Turkish women complain about not being allowed to work, Ellison points to the equally problematic situation for British workers who "have to work" but suffer high rates of unemployment (196). The late nineteenth-century British novelist George Gissing wrote about the shortage of men in England—the remaining "odd women" then could not rely on the economic protection of marriage, and so, for this reason, his attractive heroine refuses marriage in favour of working to educate and train women. So too, Ellison argued that Turkish women must acquire useful skills before they give up the protection of the harem; and job training was indeed being initiated by reformers like Halide Edib, who helped set up and run the Red Crescent facilities. Complaining about not being able to find anyone to sew for her, Ellison writes: "It is not when women are actually starving that one can teach them a trade" (88). But the protection extended to women in the harem is also different from Western paternalism as it indicates a social organization, the legacy of Islam, that is not as relentlessly individualistic as the capitalist West and extends to a more general community, including in its reach not just women but also the poor. Thus Ellison points out that, for instance, beggars in Turkey, rather than forced into stealing as in the less charitable West, are given food and shelter and are able to retain their dignity and humanity (90).

One of the most interesting and innovative aspects of Ellison's work is this dialogue she sets up between Eastern and Western versions of feminism, allowing the practices of one to shed light on and comment on the other. Ironically, given that as she writes Europe and Turkey are on the brink of war, Ellison suggests the point of this exchange is to prevent war: "making the nations of a country understand one another better" would make armed conflict "much less possible" (156). Although, at points, she slips into the very Orientalism she is working against, as when she refers to the "awakening of a people after centuries of sleep" (62) and makes her somewhat patronizing plea to British feminists to better understand Turkish women who turn to the British for "guidance" and "example" (18), she generally works against the grain of colonialism suggesting, for instance, that Turkish women have an innovative and fresh perspective on many subjects that she would not even have been able to discuss with her more conventional English friends. Rather than assuming Britain's superiority, she asks her home country to be reflexive, interjecting with the very provocative comment: "'See,' says Europe, 'how the Turk treats his women.' 'See,' I might answer, 'how the British Government treats its women'" (80). And this is one of the ways Turkish and British feminism differ, as the Turkish had both the government and many men on their side, whereas British suffragists were often subject to public ridicule and strongly opposed. Ellison's envious approval of the "'feminist' Military Governor of Constantinople" Cemal Bey's encouragement of female participation in public spaces, even directing the police to protect them, stands in direct and unflattering, comparison to the British government who were imprisoning suffragists and as reported, in 1909 in her own paper the *Daily Telegraph*, force-feeding them with tubes when they staged hunger strikes. Although this brutality initially raised some public sympathy, by the time Ellison was in Turkey, it had drastically declined as militant suffragists, receiving no support from Parliament, were driven to extreme acts. The notorious "Black Friday" of November 18, 1913, when a six hour riot outside the Houses of Parliament saw police in pitched battles with suffragists, occurred at precisely the point when Ellison was commentating from Istanbul. This is the context in which she wrote appreciatively of the evolutionary as opposed to revolutionary nature of feminist campaigning taking place in Turkey.

Another reason, however, for the government support of women in Turkey is that the long held Western stereotypes of the oppressed Eastern female or "captive of the harem," that Ellison herself is working actively to dispel, turned the figure of the veiled woman into a battleground for competing interests. The veil has never been singular in meaning and has been adopted for reasons as diverse as such things as weather, fashion, religion, and class and Ellison herself notes the differences between city and rural veiling, commenting on the yellow embroideries that adorn the hair and shoulders of village women (148). However the veil took on a very specific set of meanings during the height of Western imperialism and the subsequent national liberation movements that followed in its wake. Westerners often portrayed the systems of veiling and segregation as symptomatic of the sickness of the "Oriental" mind, and the "degradation" of women was often used as a rational for colonial occupation. For instance, in the nineteenth century, Lord Cromer, the consul general of Egypt, adopted a "feminist" rhetoric as he condemned the "Oriental" for his treatment of women (he himself was a founding member of the anti-suffragist league in England) and the French in Algeria campaigned on a similar platform of rescuing the veiled woman from her own culture. More recently we have seen this same narrative in the recent war in Afghanistan, which was fought, at least partly, in the name of "women's rights," which foregrounded the issue of "liberating" women from the burqa. So too depictions of the oppression of Eastern women was a common theme in travel literature and as Ellison points out "unwholesome stories" about the harem and veiling sold books. For instance, Lady Annie Brassey (see this series), despite her own resistance to British suffrage and support of the British Empire, wrote: "It is a great mistake of the Turks to think that they can educate their wives and daughters, and still keep them in confinement and subjection" (79). The treatment of women, particularly veiling and segregation, thus became the focus of the violent condemnation of Muslim cultures by the West. Meanwhile in Istanbul, Cemal Paşa, recently appointed as Minister of Public Works, when asked by Ellison about his continued support for extending women's rights, directs his answer to the West with a question of his own: "this whole Eastern question, is it not a woman's question?" (82).

In response to these Western stereotypes, women and the veil took on a particular significance as Turkey was emerging as an independent nation. There were those who campaigned for the re-veiling of women as a sign of resistance to cultural imperialism and those who encouraged their unveiling as a mark of civilization, progress, and modernization. This complicated imperialist legacy thus connects feminism and nationalism in Turkey in a manner very different from British feminism. Ellison refers to the Turkish woman as "a true patriot" (78) and even ventures so far as to suggest that in this new Turkey veiling is much more a question of race and national identity than religion (110). Further, Ellison, countering the fallacy of Orientalist stereotypes, points out that not only are Turkish men not keeping women veiled and hindering their progress as is so often reported in Western sources, but they are in the foreground of the movement for their emancipation. Atatürk, a prominent member of the Committee of Union and Progress at the time of Ellison's visit, would, as the leader of the country, emerge as one of the most vocal supporters of ridding Turkey of the veil and Ellison would return in 1922 as one of the first Westerners to interview him from his base in the new capital, Ankara.

THE TRAVELLER AND HER SUBJECTS: AUTHORITY, STATUS, AND CLASS IN THE HAREM

Ellison's title puts herself, the "Englishwoman," centre-stage, and her account of her Ottoman experiences inevitably involves elements of self-presentation. During the course of the book she appears in several potentially contradictory guises: as photographic subject and as photographer; as skilled researcher and as ignorant visitor; as adroit at cross cultural dressing (skilful enough to pass as Turkish in the tomb at Eyoub) and as hopelessly gauche at mastering harem etiquette (forgetting to return the salutations of visitors, 53). Her writing and self-presentation draw on diverse literary codes and research methods, shifting uneasily between registers in ways that indicate the contradictions inherent in reporting on another culture. This is often seen in the ways that a personal tone enters into descriptions that ostensibly aim at the "scientific" status of ethnography. So too the inclusion of photographs was a common aspect of travel literature from the late nineteenth century on (see, for instance, Brassey and Dodd in this series). Many of these works relied on the stock photography that catered to Orientalist tastes and emphasized the picturesque nature of the Orient and its inhabitants. As with her writing, Ellison breaks with this convention, inserting herself into the picture by both particularizing her experiences in the harem and disrupting Orientalist notions about it. She often took her own photographs, some of which were rejected by British publishers because they did not sufficiently meet Orientalist expectations, such as her photograph of a contemporary harem that was spurned by a British newspaper because it showed too much modern European furniture. She subsequently took great delight in publishing this photograph as part of Zeyneb Hanoum's book, along with a disdainful riposte about the ignorance of the editor concerned.

Ellison's reporting does not presume to originate from the universalising perspective typical of ethnography: her accounts are clearly from a female point of view and they often destabilise Western assumptions. Whilst her account, for example, of the funeral rites for Fâtima's father gives details of burial procedure in a manner that owes allegiance to conventions of ethnographic description, these typical "manners and customs" segments are not presented as objective fact. The discussion of mourning rituals in Fatima's household is explicitly comparative and evaluative, but not always to the West's advantage: "we Westerners, with our curious ideas of Eastern life, cannot imagine the picturesque, simple, and natural attitudes the Turks have towards death" (50). Rather than naturalise a Western world view, the non-normativity of Western habits is highlighted by the reported speech of an Ottoman respondent, whose critique of Western ways is clear—"the money you people in the West spend on funeral pomp we give to the poor assembled round the grave" (51).

The conversation with this respondent also provides an opportunity for Ellison to discourse at length on the innate "democracy" of Ottoman social relations—in the household and in society as a whole—demonstrating her willingness to privilege a non-Western social structure. The lack of "snobbery" among Ottoman society is a theme often commented on by Western visitors, just as its obverse—the lack of cross-class interaction in Western society—is perplexing and conspicuous to Middle Eastern visitors to Europe (see Zeyneb Hanoum, in this series). But Ellison's approval of Ottoman class mingling rarely fails to emphasise that this is a system in which everyone "knows her part." The poor may never be forgotten, the princess may suddenly "rise and throw her arms around the neck of her *nourrice* [wet-nurse], who walks about amongst the highest of the Court ladies," but the woman of the lower orders knows that "her place is on the floor" and will refuse a chair "even though the high-born woman invites her sit" (45–55). If the Western visitor to an elite household likely finds it difficult to identify rank because the usual Western signifiers of dress and etiquette are not in place, the local population understands precisely who is who. By decoding the social hierarchy of the harem space Ellison displaces Orientalist readings of the harem as a sexually saturated domain outside of social relations, but she also reveals how her understanding of harem society is determined by her own pleasure in the luxury and ennoblement it offers her. The book is full of references to the gracious consideration shown to her by her Ottoman hosts, who place her in the best seats, rise whenever she enters the room, endlessly offer her coffee and food, lend her their best clothes, expect her to stay for as long as possible, and generally do everything possible to ensure her comfort.

While travel often allowed Western women, commonly treated as honorary men in their travels abroad, to indulge in liberties not generally afforded them in their home countries, these liberties are also often dependent on both their privileged class positions and their assumed dominant position in relation to the other cultures, and, in particular, to the other women they encountered. In contrast, Ellison emphatically avoids such denigrations of local femininity: whilst she adores the elevated social position she attains in the Ottoman dominions, she celebrates her (partial) immersion into female society and never represents local women as silent or passive. If her Western privileges give her access to male dignitaries, she is also just as quick to list the prominent women that she meets.

One of the markers of respect paid to Ellison in Fâtima's harem was the assignment to her of her own slave, whom she renamed "Miss Chocolate." Her account of their relationship provides a mechanism for talking about the specificity of the Ottoman slave trade—a subject that many Western and nearly all Middle Eastern women writers felt compelled to cover, since they knew that Western readers presumed the Ottoman system to be the same as Atlantic and North American plantation slavery. The Ottoman slave trade had by this period reduced dramatically, and had rarely been directed to mass agricultural labour. Apart from male slaves for the military, the majority of Ottoman slaves were women intended specifically for elite harems. Slavery was not, as was the case in the West, considered a lifelong social status, nor did it prohibit attaining a position of substantial personal power and autonomy. The Islamic system encouraged manumission (after a period of service, or on marriage), whilst the slave origin of many women in the Turko-Circassian elite was not a matter of shame—Circassian girls were often held to prefer the chance of life in a luxury harem to the arduous life of a peasant in their native mountains. For the West, the social mobility of the enslaved and once-enslaved was extremely troubling, and, in wanting to explain how Ottoman slavery was not as the West imagined, Ellison was in part countering Western ignorance. Ellison's notations on the generally benign treatment of household slaves, whose lot she compares favourably to the mistreatment of domestic servants at home, can be read in this light.

But having one's own slave could not be without anxieties, and her book creates a range of appellations for "Miss Chocolate" and her peers that slips them bewilderingly between free and un-free status. Introducing Miss Chocolate initially as "my maid of the moment, Cadhem Hair Calfat" we learn directly that "(Calfat means slave)," neatly deferring the un-free status of her servant to a matter of translation (10). "Miss Chocolate," as Ellison has taken it upon herself to rename her, is subsequently referred to variously as "my chocolate coloured attendant," "my negress," and as a slave, whilst the other slave women in the household often appear simply as "domestics." Although she does regularly call a slave a slave, Ellison's mix of titles for those labouring in the household reveals more than simply her own discomfort about their enslavement. Her narrative reflects the difficulty faced by many outsiders in comprehending the status of women in elite harems during a period when slavery had been formally banned by the Young Turks in 1908, and had been in the decades before the revolution increasingly uncommon. When Ellison writes of Miss Chocolate "by degrees I shall find out her life history, as I shall find out, perhaps, before I go, the names and social status of all these women here," her caution that "I shall have to work slowly and carefully, lest my sympathetic interest should be mistaken for idle curiosity" (26) shows an awareness of the intrusiveness of ethnographic enquiry and the clashing cultural codes that impeded a clear recognition of social relations. In reminding her readers that many of the women serving in the house had been formally manumitted but elected to stay on as servants/retainers, Ellison is attempting to explain a social status that to Westerners seemed liminal, but that was to locals easily recognisable. But the ways in which Ellison compares slavery with domestic service is not just a criticism of Western self-satisfaction. It also melds with her defence of the harem system as one that offers "protection" to women, unlike the difficulties of finding respectable and sufficiently remunerated employment in the Western market economies.

CONCLUSION: RECEPTION AND LEGACY

Although Ellison has been largely neglected, her work offers an important intervention in both feminism and Orientalism, and she is a pivotal figure in this series, which considers to what extent dialogues can been carried on across and against national, racial, and class boundaries. Ellison's willingness to set British and Turkish, Christian and Islamic, systems and customs against each other, weighing each for their value, offered a refreshing perspective in the field of travel literature, which had been dominated by an Orientalism that had assumed, for the most part, the superiority of British ways. Her determinedly feminist focus on, support of, and empathy with Turkish women also set her apart from those female travel writers who used their status as foreigners to access the harem as a means of penetrating it. Much to the horror of their Eastern hostesses, such writers often offered the harem up as spectacle to their Western audiences, complimenting rather than disrupting the work of their male Orientalist counterparts. It is for this reason that many of the harems closed their doors to Western visitors. Ellison, however, rather than silencing Ottoman women, collaborates with them to create venues for their voices, incorporating testimonial from Ottoman respondents in her book, and using her publishing contacts to introduce both

Melek Hanoum's and Zeyneb Hanoum's works to a Western audience.

Although Ellison seemingly downplays and undercuts her own authority, as she does, for example, in the introduction to this book, by positioning her work as "only an Englishwoman's impressions of Turkish harem life, written during a very happy and interesting visit amongst Turkish friends," she was someone whose opinions had considerable weight at home and in Turkey (vii). Well connected with the upper echelons of Ottoman political and social circles, Ellison's writing extended her reach to a wider public, with some of her *Daily Telegraph* articles translated in the CUP paper *Tanin* (for which Halide Edib wrote regularly). This international status was not lost on British observers, and the *Daily Telegraph*'s Istanbul correspondent when reporting in 1914 that Ottoman women had won the right to take selected classes at the university in Istanbul credited Ellison's "deeply psychological articles"—the very insight she denies in this book—with having "done not a little towards raising the status of Turkish women" (11). This up to the minute contemporaneity and immersion in local politics marks Ellison's writing as distinct from previous models of harem literature. In this and other ways her introduction of a professional, journalistic, and explicitly political dimension pioneered changes in the wider field of women's travel literature. In her *Telegraph* articles, even more than in the book version of *An Englishwoman in a Turkish Harem*, Ellison commented frequently on details of British foreign policy, often vehemently putting the Turkish case against "commonsense" British assumptions. When, in 1914, the British government appeared to be about to back Greek claims on the Aegean island of Mitylene (left to the arbitration of the Great Powers in the Treaty of London, March 1913), Ellison remonstrated angrily:

> Has Sir Edward Grey ever stopped for five minutes
> to think what that means? An Island five kilometers
> from the Turkish coast to be given to the Greeks? It
> is as if some foreign Power had ordered us to hand
> over the Isle of Wight to the Germans! Was that
> decision made without even looking at the map?
>
> *Daily Telegraph* February 6, 1914, p. 7

Breaking new ground for women writers by intervening publicly in the macro-politics of foreign policy, Ellison also demonstrates her feminist credentials by directly linking international events to the ostensibly micro-political domain of gender relations. Refusing to separate the situation of women from the political domain, she counters in the *Daily Telegraph* requests from "a correspondent" for predictions on the "future for Turkish women" with the riposte that the war which is bound to follow from ceding territory to Greece makes it impossible to "speak optimistically of the future" of the country, let alone its women (7).

In the ways that Ellison crossed harem literature with political and ethnographic reportage, she, along with her much more renowned contemporary—the traveler, archeologist, and Arabist, Gertrude Bell (1868–1926)—opened up the field to women who wanted to stake out careers in the Middle East. Both Ellison's feminism and her anti-Orientalist stance, however, set her apart from Bell, who, during the First World War, worked for British intelligence and helped to organize the Arabs against the Turks. The Arabs, though, were being betrayed by the West, even as they fought against the Ottoman Empire, by the secret Franco-British Sykes-Picot agreement to establish between them a mandate over much of the Middle East. Ellison shared more in common with Dame Freya Stark (1893–1993), one of the most famed female travelers in the Middle East, who also relied on writing to fund her exploits since grants were largely reserved for men. The fame her books brought Stark did eventually lead to grants from the Royal Geographical Society, and she also worked as an advisor to the British government during the Second World War, but she, like Ellison, remained critical of British imperialism in the Middle East. After *An Englishwoman in a Turkish Harem*, Ellison's profile continued to rise and in 1922 she was the first British woman to receive permission to cross enemy lines and visit the nationalist camp at Ankara during the War of Independence. Her interviews there with Mustafa Kemal and others in the nationalist leadership, published in *An Englishwoman in Angora*, were repeated on her next trip in 1927 when she revisited Ankara as the new capital of the Turkish Republic, which led to her publication *Turkey To-day*. Despite her impressive career, however, unlike Bell and Stark, her work and name have virtually disappeared from the historical record.

It is in these later publications that Ellison reveals herself to be more partisan. In her unwavering support of Atatürk and his promotion of state-sponsored feminism, she seems untroubled by his increasing suppression of the autonomous women's movement, even though these were precisely the groups of Ottoman women reformers that she praises so highly in *An Englishwoman in a Turkish Harem*. She was similarly forgiving of Atatürk's autocracy and establishment of single party rule, such as was to lead to the "exile" of Halide Edib. Ellison's willingness to overlook his government's suppression of ethnic minorities, like the Kurds, is an extension of her marginalization of minority populations in her 1915 account—though here she is deliberately challenging the Western tendency to side uncritically with Christian opponents of the Ottomans, be they Bulgarians outside the Empire or Armenians within it. In 1928, a reviewer of *Turkey To-day* in the *Times Literary Supplement* was critical of the fact that she seemed to disregard the suffering of a population who had "toiled to release the country from the absolutism of a Sultan" only to find themselves under the control of a "new autocracy" (719). Nonetheless, her reviewer cannot deny that she has "a good deal of experience of the country, both as it used to be and as it is now," and the "additional advantage of having also seen it in the transitional stage between past and present." Ellison's unique and varied experience of Turkey gives her status as an expert respondent, even if the reviewer dislikes her opinions.

Negotiating relationships across cultural boundaries, operating professionally at the borders of different literary fields, managing publishing projects internationally, and maintaining personal loyalties in times of extreme political instability, Grace Ellison reflects on and criticizes her own country's economic, gender, and foreign politics. However, in doing so she also resists the Orientalist trap of reifying the other and going "native" as she remains, determinedly, an "Englishwoman" in a Turkish harem.

WORKS CITED

Brassey, Lady Annie. *Sunshine and Storm in the East or Cruises to Cyprus and Constantinople.* (1881). Introd. Scott A. Leonard. Piscataway, NJ: Gorgias Press 2004.

Dodd, Anna Bowman. *In the Palaces of the Sultan.* (1903). Introd. Teresa Heffernan. Piscataway, NJ: Gorgias Press 2004.

Ellison, Grace. "Life in the Harem." *Daily Telegraph* 6 February 1914.

———. *The Disadvantages of Being a Woman.* London: A. M. Philpot Ltd. 1923.

"Turkey To-Day." *Times Literary Supplement* 11 October 1928.

"Woman in Turkey." *Daily Telegraph* 9 February 1914.

Zeyneb Hanoum. *A Turkish Woman's European Impressions.* (1913). Ed. Gace Ellison. Introd. Reina Lewis. Piscataway, NJ: Gorgias Press 2004.

Notes on the Plates

When Grace Ellison's book *An Englishwoman in a Turkish Harem* first appeared in 1915 it contained thirteen photographic illustrations. These were a significant feature of the book and were announced on the fly-leaf by her British publisher (Methuen) as something that would attract the potential reader or purchaser. However, as we discuss in the introduction to this volume, Ellison has fallen into obscurity in the last several decades and copies of her book are extremely rare. This is one of the reasons why she is reprinted here as part of *Cultures in Dialogue*. It was exceptionally difficult to find a copy of the original book available to use for reproduction and in the end we had to compromise and use an American edition published by McBride, Nash and Co. Although the American edition appeared the same year (1915) it did not include the photographs. The fact that her book appeared immediately with an American imprint testifies to the importance given to Ellison in her lifetime, and it may have been that the absence of the photographs allowed a cheaper price so as to reach a wider market.

We did not want to reprint this book without the images. We have thus added the photographs, sourced separately. The written component is exactly the same, page for page, as the British first edition. Pasting the illustrations throughout the text at this stage would have resulted in changes to the pagination, so we have kept them separate at the front. In order to give a sense of how the photographs interlink with the written narrative we have included the original list of illustrations that gives the details of the pages between which they would have originally been inserted.

Whilst we regret that we could not maintain the integrity of the first edition in this facsimile reproduction, we hope that this arrangement will cause a minimum of disruption to Grace Ellison's new readers.

We would never have found an illustrated copy of Ellison's book without the help of the librarians at Saint Mary's University in Halifax and those at the Rare Books and Special Collections Division at McGill University in Montreal. We wish especially to thank them for their persistence in this quest.

Teresa Heffernan & Reina Lewis

List of Illustrations

HALIDÉ HANOUM, THE BEST KNOWN TURKISH WOMEN WRITERS AND A LEADER
OF THE WOMAN'S MOVEMENT

MISS "CHOCOLATE"

AN ENGLISHWOMAN WEARING A YASHMAK

H.E. GENERAL DJEMAL PASHA, MARINE MINISTER.
THE FEMINIST MINISTER

H.E. TALAAT BEY, MINISTER OF THE INTERIOR.
A SUPPORTER OF THE WOMAN'S MOVEMENT

A CONTRIBUTOR TO THE NEW TURKISH WOMAN'S PAPER "KANDINLAR DUNYASSI"
("THE FEMININE WORLD")

DANCING CLASS AT THE GIRLS' SCHOOL, BROUSSA

THE GREEN MOSQUE AT BROUSSA

BROUSSA

THE FOOTBALL TEAM AT THE BROUSSA LYCEE

OPENING OF THE BELGIAN SCHOOL OF ARTS AND CRAFTS, STAMBOUL.

TURKISH LADIES IN THE COUNTRY WITH THEIR EUROPEAN GOVERNESSES

I DEDICATE
THESE LETTERS TO ALL THOSE
WHO MADE MY VISIT
SO INTERESTING AND HAPPY,
BUT PARTICULARLY TO MY FRIEND
AND HOSTESS.

PREFACE

THESE letters do not claim to be a psychological study of Turkish character, nor are they a political or historical treatise. They are only an Englishwoman's impressions of Turkish harem life, written during a very happy and interesting visit amongst Turkish friends. Should I not have said in these letters what my Turkish sisters expected me to say; should I not have understood their civilization as they hoped I would understand it; I feel sure they will forgive one who they know has always been, and will always be their sincere friend. To correct the errors, prejudice, and hatred which have become almost part of the British national "attitude" towards Turkey is not an easy task. If these letters have been able in ever so small a way to spread some of the enthusiasm and love I feel for a nation which Europe has so severely censured, they will at least have justified the reason of their existence.

My thanks are due to the editor of the *Daily Telegraph* for allowing me to reproduce those letters which have appeared in the columns of that paper.

GRACE ELLISON

ROUEN, 1915

CONTENTS

ix

INTRODUCTION

AS one who for nearly forty years has been a friend and admirer of the Turks and a student of their language and literature, it is a satisfaction to me, especially in the dark days through which Turkey has passed and is passing, to find a fresh opportunity of testifying to my belief in the virtues of that much-maligned and ill-used race. I have, therefore, willingly acceded to the request of the authoress of this work that I should add to it, now that it is finished, a few words of introduction, though such introduction, as it seems to me, is hardly needed. Miss Ellison enjoyed an opportunity of seeing an aspect of Turkish life which few English women and no English men have been privileged to study at first hand, and, as her book abundantly shows, she has made good use of her opportunity. It will not be her fault if she fails to " correct the errors, prejudice and hatred which have become almost part of the British national attitude towards Turkey," and " to spread some of the enthusiasm and love " she feels " for a nation which Europe has so severely censured."

Before the Revolution of 1908 Turkish family
life and the qualities of the Turkish woman were,
in all save the rarest cases, sealed books even
to those Europeans who mixed freely with Turks
and spoke Turkish with fluency; and though
since that period a few Turkish ladies, notably
the talented authoress, Hálida Hanoum (to whom
Miss Ellison repeatedly refers in the course of
these pages),[1] have visited England, and even
pursued their studies with remarkable success in
English women's colleges, they are still sufficiently unknown and surrounded with mystery to
give to this present book a real interest and
value. On one occasion, some four years ago,
when I was at Constantinople, I was invited to
meet a group of Turkish ladies who were anxious
to make the acquaintance of an Englishman who
had studied their language and literature, edited
the most comprehensive and sympathetic history
of their poetry,[2] and was known to them as a
sincere friend of their country and their religion.
I was much struck by their eagerness and intelli-

---

[1] Pp. 17, 66, 69, 77, 107.

[2] The late Mr. E. J. W. Gibb's *History of Ottoman Poetry*.
Mr. Gibb died on December 5, 1901, little more than a year after
the publication of the first volume of this great work. The remaining five volumes, of which the last (vol. vi) contained the
Turkish originals of the poems translated in vols. i–v, were edited
by myself, at the request of his widow and parents, from the carefully written and well-arranged manuscript materials which were
found amongst his papers. A seventh volume, dealing with the
most modern period, is in course of preparation.

gence, as well as by the distinction of their manners, and I am glad to find the impression left on my mind by this single occasion entirely confirmed by Miss Ellison's much more extended experience. Knowing how absurd and baseless are many of the opinions about the Turks and Islam entertained in Europe (so that, to take one instance only, people who ought to know better constantly re-assert the oft-repeated calumny that in the Mohammedan faith the existence of a soul is denied to women), I was prepared to find Turkish ladies much more intelligent and better educated than is generally supposed; but the reality greatly exceeded my expectations. Of their profound patriotism Miss Ellison gives (on pp. 85-87) a moving example, and Mr. Morgan Shuster, at pp. 188-9 of his great book, *The Strangling of Persia*, has shown that in this quality the Persian women do not fall short of their Turkish sisters.

Nothing has so greatly retarded the evolution of the Muslim nations as the backwardness of their women, seeing that in the formation of the children's characters it is nearly always the mother who plays the chief part. Polygamy, as Miss Ellison points out, is so much rarer than is generally supposed in Europe, save in the wealthiest classes and especially in the royal household, that its evils have probably been exaggerated; but, for the reasons set forth on

p. 96 of this book, happy and suitable marriages
are rarer in the East than in Europe. The changes
in this respect which are now taking place, and
with which this book largely deals, are not the
least of the blessings conferred by the Revolution of 1908, and though it is at present the
fashion in the English press to disparage that
revolution, which was at first hailed with so much
apparent enthusiasm, I cannot understand how
any one who knew Turkey both before and
after it can deny or ignore the vast improve-
ment which it has effected not only in the
happiness but in the moral and intellectual
condition of the people. In our own country
the contemplation of a Liberalism which takes
Tsardom as its ideal, a Conservatism which coquets
with lawlessness and makes two such reactionary
measures as Conscription and Protection, the
chief "constructive features" of its programme,
a Cabinet which pays less and less heed to Parliament, a Parliament which grows ever less and less
in touch with public opinion, and a Press which
tends increasingly to make the selection rather
than the collection of news its main object,
has produced a political pessimism, the like of
which few living men can remember, which makes
it difficult for us to believe in the reality of any
political enthusiasm, or to understand what
emancipation means to a people who have just
emerged from centuries of despotism. The bright

hopes born in Turkey in 1908 and in Persia two
years earlier have, indeed, been sorely dimmed,
when not entirely extinguished, less through the
faults or shortcomings of the patriotic elements in
these countries than through the Machiavellian
cynicism and materialistic greed of the Great
Powers of Europe, who least of all desired any real
reform in the lands which they had already marked
down for their spoliation. Yet even should Turkey
and Persia unhappily perish and cease to be counted
amongst the free and independent nations of the
world, the historians of the future will pay the
tribute of admiration withheld by the politicians
and journalists of to-day to their last splendid
struggles for freedom, independence, and reform.
For truly says one of the Arabian poets :

Kam máta qawm^{un} wa má mátat makárimu-hum,
Wa 'ásha qawm^{un} wa hum fi'n-nási amwátu !

"Many a people's virtues survive when themselves are sped,
And many a people linger who are counted by men as dead !"

It cannot, of course, be denied that the Turkish
reformers (much more, in my opinion, than the
Persians) made several frightful mistakes, the
worst of which was the vain and disastrous
attempt to Turkify or Ottomanize the various
non-Turkish elements of the Ottoman Empire,
a matter in which their policy contrasted very
unfavourably with that pursued by the late Sultan

b

'Abd-ul-Hamíd. This grievous error, like many lesser ones, was largely due, in my opinion, to the French influences which played so large a part, both in the political and the literary field, in the evolution of the " New Turks " (*Yeñi Turkler*), or, as they are commonly though absurdly styled (now even by themselves) " Young Turks." The French are, indeed, more chauvinistic, more intolerant of languages, customs and ideas other than their own, in a word more " insular," than the English; and from the time of Kemál and Shinásí, the founders of the " Young Turkish " school, until that of Ahmed Rizá Bey, Dr. Názim, 'Alí Kemál, and others who took a prominent part in recent events, French ideas have dominated the Turkish reformers. So, just as the French discourage the use of the Breton language in Brittany, and endeavour to impose their own tongue on the inhabitants of that Celtic province, the " Young Turks " endeavoured to impose their language on the Arabs and Armenians, and their alphabet on the Albanians, while at the same time, with a strange inconsistency, they were ruining the Turkish language by hasty and ill-considered attempts to " reform " its spelling and to modify or even entirely change the Arabic characters in which, like all other Muhammadan languages, it is written.

I agree so entirely with nearly everything that

Miss Ellison says as to the true democracy[1] and hospitality[2] of the Turks, their kindness to the poor,[3] their sincerity and unceremoniousness, the humane character of the "slavery," with the toleration of which they have been reproached, and the like, that it seems ungracious to dissent from a statement which she makes on pp. 104–5 as to the New School of Turkish poetry. She quotes an opinion as to the value of this modern poetry expressed by my late friend, Mr. E. J. W. Gibb (than whom in all that concerns Turkish literature no greater authority can be adduced), for which I also appear to be made responsible, as also, perhaps, for the preceding implication that the Turks often excelled their earlier Persian exemplars. This, I feel bound to state, is not my view. Whatever comparisons may be instituted between the Turks and Persians, and in whatever points the former may be deemed superior to the latter, in literary skill and poetic talent there can, in my opinion, be no comparison whatever. Turkish poetry, whether old or new, is at best seldom more than pretty and graceful, while often the verses of even comparatively unknown Persian poets (let alone such masters of the art as Jalálu'd Dín Rúmí, Sa'dí, Háfiz and Jámí) touch the sublime. The production of fine poetry may not be the highest aim of man, or the object for which he was created, but, what-

---

[1] Pp. 21, 45, 54.   [2] P. 22.   [3] P. 52.

ever this distinction may be worth, some of the
finest poetry in the world has been produced by
the Persians, and no one, I think, however
great an admirer of the Turks he may be, could
make this assertion about them.

In what concerns the languages and literatures
of Western and Central Asia, I must, I fear,
admit that I am what my learned and versatile
Turkish friend, Dr. Rizá Tevfiq, sometime
Deputy of Adrianople in the Ottoman Parliament,
and commonly known in Turkey as " *Feylesúf
Rizá* " (" Rizá the Philosopher "), calls Mu'allim
Nájí, the last great champion of the old or
classical style in Turkey, " *un réactionnaire
décidé*," and it is with certain tendencies of the
" Young Turks " in this domain of philology and
letters that I find myself least in sympathy. I
have already alluded to certain innovations in
spelling which appear to me deplorable, and to
several still more deplorable attempts to modify
or abolish that beautiful Arabian character which
is one of the strongest bonds uniting all Muhammadan nations ; and I must add a few words of
disapproval of that fantastic movement, briefly
referred to on pp. 67–8 of this book, known as
" The New Turanian " (*Yeñi Túrán*). Against
the attempts of this school to revive the use of
obsolescent Turkish words and to displace in
their favour the equivalent, and at present much
more familiar, Persian and Arabic vocables, I

have nothing to say; there is no more reason
why a Turk should not endeavour to persuade
his countrymen to call God " *Tañri* " instead
of " *Alláh*," or fire " *üd* " instead of " *átesh*,"
than there is why an Englishman should not
strive to oust from his language the words
" Preface " and " Introduction " in favour of
" Foreword," or even " photograph " in favour
of " light-bild " (as some few have done), provided always that he is not so archaic and
Anglo-Saxon as to be totally unintelligible. My
objection to the " Young Turanian " School is
their hatred of Arabic and Persian culture and
desire to cut themselves altogether adrift from
them, and their grotesque ideal not merely of a
Pan-Turkish but of a Turanian world-empire,
which should exclude Arabs, Persians, and other
non-Turanian Muhammadan elements, but should
on the other hand include not only Tartars and
Mongols, but even Bulgarians. To such strange
lengths does the distorted Nationalism of these
" New Turanians " extend that they blame their
own great Sultan Báyezíd, " the Thunder-bolt,"
because, not recognizing his " Turanian over-
lord," he strove to arrest the devastating advance
of Tamerlane the Tartar, and perished in the
attempt. To me the aims of this school, so far
as I understand them, appear little less insane
than those of Marinetti and the Italian Futurists.
Far truer, saner and more reasonable is the

Pan-Islamic ideal of Sayyid Jamálu'd-Dín al-Afghání, whose body rests, after the storm and stress through which it passed, in the cemetery of Nishán-Tásh in Constantinople.

These, however, are comparatively small matters, the inevitable exuberances of a great National Awakening. However we may appraise the "Committee of Union and Progress" or the "Liberals," Enver Pasha, Tal'at, Jávíd and Ahmed Rizá on the one hand, or Kyámil Pasha, Dámád Feríd Pasha and Isma'íl Kemál on the other, let us render all honour to the noble and often nameless and fameless Turkish patriots, both men and women, who by their lives and deaths have during the last eight years striven so gallantly to save and free their country; and, when we think of their mistakes, let us remember what the Turkish poet says :—

" *Yár-siz qálir kimesné 'ayb-siz yár isteyan !* "

"Friendless surely he remaineth who demands a faultless friend !"

EDWARD G. BROWNE

CAMBRIDGE, *May 5, 1914.*

AN ENGLISHWOMAN IN
A TURKISH HAREM

AN ENGLISHWOMAN IN A TURKISH HAREM

CHAPTER I

BACK TO THE HAREM

IT is a landscape of unending and beautiful sadness which surrounds the Konak where I am now living. In my home away yonder I had imagined that where the sun shines there must be laughter and merriment, yet here, face to face with reality, the sun, the bright blue sky, and clear atmosphere have steeped everything around —the mosques, the minarets, and mournful cypress trees, which stretch towards heaven like a prayer, with that inexplicable sadness which is the basis of Oriental life.

How could I have expected to find laughter and merriment in a landscape like this? Here happiness even is expressed in some form of sadness; the people's songs of rejoicing are like funeral hymns; the sweetest poetry is sad beyond our Western comprehension; the tales the old slave tells us as we sit cross-legged round the

I

big mangol are of sadness so great that I often
wonder whence they come, and yet, paradox of
paradoxes, I have come back to Stamboul to
laugh, for I have never laughed anywhere as I
have in this land of extremes and contradictions
and surprises.

.   .   .   .   .

And now, after five years, here I am back
again enjoying once more the calm and peace of
an Eastern home, and the interesting society of
my dear friend Fâtima (I change the name). To
the Western ear, to be staying in a Turkish harem
sounds alarming, and not a little—yes, let us
confess it—improper. When, before I left my
own country, I had the imprudence to tell a
newspaper correspondent that I was longing to
get back to the quiet harem existence, I was accused of "advocating polygamy," for to the un-
initiated the word "harem" means a collection
of wives, legitimate or otherwise, and even the
initiated prefers to pretend he knows no other
meaning.

Worn out with what we in the West call pleasures of society, the fatigue of writing against
time, the rush and bustle of our big Western
capitals, the hideous and continual noise of the
traffic, which, like a great roaring wave, seems
gradually to deaden one's understanding ; how
good it is to be here !

The wonderful silence ! Sometimes it is almost
terrifying ! And at nights when I rise and peep

through the lattice windows and see the beautiful moon bathing with its silver magnificence the silent, sleeping city and the calm, quiet Marmora beyond, it is difficult to believe that there are living souls in these dimly lighted streets, and the Bekjih's tap, tap, tapping on the cobbled stones sounds, in the stillness, like some spirit rapping from another world.

Yet much as I am drinking in the beauty of my new surroundings, they do not in the least force me to write. In this wonderful garden of God, for here one feels so keenly a divine presence in every living thing, ideas surge through the brain; every nerve, every sense tingles with the beauty around; one becomes part and parcel of its grandeur, but alas! the thoughts vanish before they even come to any precision. Encircled by such Nature, how can one write? "You in your Western cities," once said to me a Dervishe of the contemplative order, "have you time or place or opportunity for contemplation?" No doubt he was right, yet, like all those Turks who are privileged to make their choice, we are dwelling on a height, and, like the Dervishe, we have time, place, and opportunity for contemplation. But do we ever get beyond contemplation?

The diary of my existence as a Turkish woman, which in England I imagined could be written in a very short while, lies day after day in the form of a pencil and exercise book, untouched, on the little mother-of-pearl table in the most comfortable corner of my large bedroom. "To-morrow," I say, like a true Turkish woman, and alas! in Turkey it takes a few to-morrows to beget "some day"; "some day" is soon changed into "never," and who knows whether the best of my Turkish impressions will not be given "their local habitation and name" in a room of some Continental hotel?

Now I understand how weeks and months, years even, may pass without receiving news from Turkish friends; now I understand that lack of what we English call "common courtesy." We have misjudged the Turks. A pen in the harem! The unnecessary intrusion! The re-forming fever which has swept over the land of Islam ever since the Constitution has not yet taught the Turkish women the use of a pen as we understand it. When I reproached my friend and hostess with not having written one letter, "Why should I write," she asked; "what have I to say? You know exactly how every moment of my life is being spent. You know my affection for you, and when two friends are really sure of one another's sympathy, each can feel the thoughts the other is thinking. . . ." And so we took up the threads of the conversation where we had left them five years ago.

Fâtima did not know I was coming to Constantinople. She was not dead, of that I was sure, so I should find her, no matter into what part of Turkey she might have wandered. But the news of my arrival reached my friend almost as soon as I had found her address. She came at once to see me at the hotel. A Turkish woman visiting me at an hotel! Was it possible? Five years ago what would not have been her punishment for such reckless *licence*? The customs of the country do not yet, however, allow Turkish women to visit hotels, and in taking every step forward she has to run the risk of offending the ignorant and fanatical mob.

Fâtima did not come in by the front entrance. Quite recently a restaurant for "ladies only" has been opened by the same management as the hotel where I stayed and is, to some extent, a rendezvous for Turkish women. It is their first step towards a "fashionable" club, and to me, the newcomer, another big step towards freedom. Let those Western critics, who have taken such a deliberate stand against the present government and declared "the new order of things worse than the old," take into consideration such details as the opening of a restaurant for Turkish women. It is part of a great scheme of reform, and everything is going on in proportion. In 1908 more than two men sitting at a café together were "suspect" and reported at headquarters; in 1913 Turkish *women* meet in a restaurant and discuss political subjects—certainly this is not the Turkey I expected to see. . . .

Having some work to finish that day, I had

given orders that I would see no one, and consequently when Fâtima asked for me in the restaurant she was told that I was ill. I was in my room writing, and at first hardly heeded a gentle knock at my door. Then came a faint repetition of the first knock, and a few minutes after followed yet another and another tap. At last I rose and opened the door to see who was there. A moment's pause, then a little black-robed, thickly veiled figure threw herself in my arms and without saying a word, without even raising her veil, just clung and clung to me. It was Fâtima, and this was our meeting after five years without having seen or even heard of one another.

" Little Fâtima," I asked, when at last our long embrace had finished, " how did you get here ? "

" I slipped through the side door and came up in the lift," she answered, and she nearly laughed her hair down at the thought of her own daring. Five years ago the zenith of Fâtima's longing was to be taken up in a hotel lift. I had begged her father to let her satisfy her curiosity—he was powerful enough to do so—but he did not say "No" and he did not say " Yes " either, and she went on wondering and longing and wondering, and now, when she least expected it, her ambition had been gratified.

It was arranged that I should go to Fâtima that very afternoon, the carriage would be sent to fetch me, and the same old coachman would drive

me from the noise, vulgarity, and " patchwork "
morality of that Pera which to me was as obnoxious
as Stamboul was delightful.

" I shall be counting the minutes till your
arrival," said Fâtima, as she rose to go, and all of
a sudden for the first time she realized that she
had not only to go back the way she came, but
face the crowd. How delightfully Turkish!
Counting the cost of the wares when the bill is in
your hand—such a contrast to our British prudence!

" But tell me, Fâtima," I said, as together we
boldly walked down the staircase and out at the
front door, " how did you like your first journey
in a lift ? "

" That you were alone and ill in an hotel," she
answered, " was of more importance than anything else. I never even thought about it."

.　　.　　.　　.　　.

The sun was shining brightly that afternoon—
shining as it only shines in the East. All the
long way from Pera to my new home it had
darted its way through the carriage windows,
showing so distinctly the thick coating of dust
which had spread itself so comfortably on my black
serge gown, and transfiguring the large white
buttons of the carriage seat into sparkling diamond
stars. At every corner I recognized old nooks—
old wisteria-covered houses, my favourite mosques
and fountains, the same slowly moving crowd,
the same beggars almost, and I was going back
to the Fâtima who had grown from a girl to a

woman—Fâtima who had so persistently resisted the European civilization at her very door, if it in any way prevented her remaining faithful to the traditions of her own civilization and religion.

.   .   .   .   .

But at last we are there.   Fâtima has come to the door to meet me and hugs me into the big salon.   There are the same tiny cigarettes, the same coffee cups, the same endless rows of bon-bon boxes filled with the delicious candies of the East, the same liqueurs, the same array of cakes, and we walk and talk as though miles and years had never separated us.

But the sun is now sinking to rest.   It is our dinner-hour, the candles are being lighted, the darlingest little baby girl toddles in to bid her mother good-night and make the acquaintance of her new "aunt."   Kissing my hand, she raises it to her forehead with the grace of a little Empress.   Dear little Perihan with the beautiful, wide-awake, brown eyes! Will your destiny be like that of the great Eastern Princess whose name you bear?

CHAPTER II

"TIME'S FOLDED WINGS"

BUT to return to the burden of letter-writing. Another Turkish friend, a lady who has stayed in England, considers one of the most disagreeable features of our civilization is our continual answering of letters. "Unnecessary letters," she called them, "and I pitied my poor hostess," she explained, "wasting the greater part of her morning choosing where she would or would not eat and asking friends to eat with her." Here our friends come uninvited, they take what we at home call "pot luck" with delightful and refreshing unceremoniousness.

But the greatest obstacle to one's writing, setting aside the atmosphere, is the lack of solitude. Here there is, except for the honoured guest, the solitude of the multitude and the silence of familiarity, but solitude, as we understand it in the West, *i.e.* one's own self within one's own room, and the door locked, never. And I doubt very much as I write these lines whether solitude and its near relative, celibacy,

9

will ever be admitted or even understood in these Eastern homes.

Several times, however, when the thought of dear friends in my home away yonder has pricked my conscience I have escaped to my room to write. But my maid for the moment, Cadhem Haïr Calfat (Calfat means slave), an elegant negress, follows me to see what she can do for me. I am seated on the sofa —she uses the word "esbab," and I understand the word "esbab" means "dress"—I shake my head. No, I will not change my dress. I hear "sou" (water). I shake my head again. I washed a short while ago. "Satch" (hair). No, my hair is quite in order. I pass my hand over my forehead, and move my fingers, to make her understand I want to write. She thinks I am ill, and runs to fetch my hostess, who hastens to find out what is wrong. She, too, fails to understand why I go to my bedroom to write in solitude when I could write at a big desk in the salon with the other ladies to keep me company.

But what a devoted creature is my chocolate-coloured attendant ! With what patience she tries to make me understand ! Not a stitch of clothing will she allow me to put on by myself, and only when I am safely tucked up under my mosquito net does she leave me alone. And what would she say now if by any chance the idea should enter her faithful woolly head to come and see whether I am all right ? Here I am, outside my mosquito net, writing by the candle light till the scratch, scratching of my pen sounds almost terrifying in this still household and the silence of the night.

The other afternoon, on returning from our afternoon drive, lady visitors arrived. Here was my opportunity to write. So, after we had drunk our coffee and smoked a cigarette, I excused myself, went upstairs, and Miss Chocolate (as my negress is now called by all my friends) removed my tcharchaff (veil and cape). By the time, however, that I could make her understand her service was finished for the moment, the sun began to set, with a magnificence only to be seen in the East. I stepped on to the balcony. From the minaret of the neighbouring mosque a clear, wonderful voice rings through the air, calling the faithful to prayer. I hear also the muezzins, in the distance, singing the Moslem credo; it is like an echo, for every note in the scale is a faint repetition of the beautiful voice which wakes me at the break of dawn with a reminder of the greatness of God—and all the while the sky is increasing in warmth, now it has formed itself into a wonderful vermilion carpet, and wrapped the mournful cypress trees and mosques and minarets which rest upon it, with a wealth of the finest azure blue, and even the wooden houses on the neighbouring hills have changed into little ochre palaces, so distinct that they seem to have been put there as an after-

thought. Then there is the beautiful Sea of
Marmora, cloaked in a mass of purple and red
and blue and gold. Could any spectacle be more
gorgeous? How well now I understand those
beings who worship the sun!

The visitors have taken their departure—they
must be home before the sun has set completely.
My friend has now joined me. On the balcony
we stand and watch in silence. We, too, have
become part of the glorious landscape; we, too,
are bathed in the wonderful roseate tints of the
setting sun. . . . The sun has set. Miss Chocolate is there, to dress me for our evening meal . . .
and my letters are still unwritten. And so the
time flies on, and we, unaware of its flight, are
happy enough. Letters belong to the West—
energy belongs to the West—but the sunset and
the dreams and the beautiful, calm felicity which I
now enjoy is the inheritance of the Woman of the
East.

But, supposing my letters are written, how
am I to post them? English letters have to be
sent from Galata. It means that a domestic
must drive to Galata and post them. That,
too, is not so easy as it sounds. I have been
trying to work out for myself this problem; if it
is the custom of this country to grant two holidays
a week to the donkey, how many are necessary
for the coachman and gardener? I look into the
garden; perhaps I see my answer in the person
of the mountainous-bodied gardener, who stands,

spade in hand, watching the flowers grow and the fruit falling from the trees. How can the inhabitants of a country of tubes and motor-'buses and telephones understand what life is like here? A distance requiring ten minutes with us would take here quite three hours, at least with Réchad, our coachman, on the box. Of him, certainly, it may be said he is merciful unto his beasts. They need not hurry unless they like ; he never whips them ; and although my friend and I together weigh less than 18 stone, the horses are allowed " a pause " at the top of each fairly steep hill.

My short stay here shows me more and more clearly how impossible it is to keep up with Western customs with all these Oriental disadvantages. For the first two or three days it may be exasperating, but the philosopher soon becomes resigned. I cannot get about if there are no means of communication, he argues, and his Western friends leave him severely alone.

The night before the Messageries Maritimes steamer arrived at Constantinople we anchored near Haidar Pasha. It was nine o'clock, but too late for the fulfilment of certain Turkish red-tapisms which make commercial life unnecessarily complicated. " See," said a diplomatist on board to me, pointing to the two shores of the Bosphorus—" Europe and Asia—action and dreams—energy and fatalism—liberty and bondage." And the lights from the European shore were shedding their brilliance on to the cool, calm

Bosphorus, and Stamboul, my present home, showed in the distance only a few flickering sparks to remind us that these good, honest Turks were yet alive, and that even in this twentieth century they had ignored the civilization which had taken possession of the greater part of their capital.

To be cut off from the society of Pera, however, with few exceptions, is no deprivation for the Turkish woman. She dislikes the women, perhaps, even more than the men, because she knows them better, but she lumps them all, both sexes and all nations, into the somewhat contemptuous term *Perote*. She dislikes the loud voices of the women—she, who is taught as the most elementary form of good breeding to speak in a soft, low voice (the domestics here literally whisper)—she dislikes the Perote's abominable habit of asking questions (for the Turkish woman will not be questioned); she dislikes the inquisitive, staring men, who look as if they would "gimlet" their way through the black face-veil the Turkish women wear. . . .

"But why do you Turkish women dislike the Perotes?" I asked one day. "They have the blood of six nations in their veins and the soul of none," replied my friend; "and the vices of the six and the virtues of none," and I have found out recently that it is these Levantines who have told the world the little that is known of Turkish women.

The veiled Turkish woman is always a source of unending interest. A chapter, at least, on harem life will always add to the value of the book; for the word "harem" stirs the imagination, conjures up for the reader visions of houris veiled in the mystery of ages, of Grand Viziers clad in many-coloured robes and wearing turbans the size and shape of pumpkins, and last, but not least, is supplied for the reader's imagination a polygamous master of the harem, and they have made him the subject of their coarsest smoking-room jokes. Poor Turks! How we have humiliated them! The Turk loves his home and he loves his wife. He is an indulgent husband and a kind father. And yet we judge him from the books which are written, not to extend the truth about a people, but only to sell; the West expects to hear unwholesome stories when it reads of the Eastern homes, and all these falsehoods are put into circulation by expelled governesses and Perote ladies, who have given an ugly form and soul to all that passes behind the door through which they are rarely privileged to enter.

Indirectly the proclamation of the Constitution has meant much to the Turkish woman. After that date she was allowed to travel and see for herself the lands about which she had read so much. Then it was with her observant eyes and receptive mind she understood our lives as no Western woman has been able to understand the East, and the result is that to-day, although to the tourist she appears as veiled and secluded as ever, yet she has advanced so rapidly that I, after an absence of five years, scarcely know her.

"It is an ill wind that blows nobody good," says our proverb, and poor consolation though it seems, it is heavy misfortune which has been the lot of poor Turkey, which has banded the women together, brought out all their best qualities and determined them, with Western militancy, to save their Fatherland at all costs.

It is time Europe saw the Turkish woman as she really is; saw her splendidly organized Red Crescent Society, her woman's paper edited by a woman, her programme for the national health, for the training of nurses and doctors, and even telephone clerks, for the near future. Surely, honour should be given where honour is due, and although, for reasons I will explain later, it will be some time before the Turkish woman can or before it would be wise for her to cast aside the veil, she is not what Europe generally imagines she is. She has awakened from the darkness and horror of the Hamidian régime with a courage and determination to show the world that one sex cannot govern a country, that the woman's voice must be heard in every matter of importance—not in the anonymous manner of yore, but openly and honestly and above-board, as is her right—and that if one sex is to be kept in ignorance it shall not be the women.

I have faith in the women of Turkey. With education—for these women, though of great culture, are not educated—they will acquire the necessary perseverance and exactitude, the lack of which keeps the Turkish woman behind the rest of Europe. With improved means of communication and organized work, too, her character will develop. She can take her place splendidly in a big cause. Whence she acquires her extraordinary courage, sangfroid, and savoir faire I do not know, but it is the details that worry her; she loses patience, and that terrible " To-morrow I will do it," which is partly due to the climate and partly the inheritance of ages, has been till now the Turkish woman's stumbling-block in all she undertakes.

I asked Halidé-Hanoum, perhaps the most active and best known of modern Turkish women, in the name of one of our prominent suffrage societies, how we English women could help the Turkish women in their advancement. " Ask them," she said, "to delete for ever that misunderstood word ' harem,' and speak of us in our Turkish ' homes.' Ask them to try and dispel the nasty atmosphere which a wrong meaning of that word has cast over our lives. Tell them what our existence really is."

And so here I am in the heart of Stamboul, a Turkish woman for the time being. Only by living the life of another people can we have any idea of the real value of that people. By

2

sinking for a while one's own personality one obtains the recompense of superior knowledge, and I have been received in a Turkish home and offered hospitality it would be difficult to equal in any other land.

Halidé-Hanoum paid a very pretty compliment to the energy, indomitable courage, and self-sacrifice of so many of the women of my country. If, then, the Eastern women can understand the tactics of a section of women workers which so many men and women of my own country have covered with ridicule and injustice, surely we in England should try to understand better the Turkish women, for it is to us they still turn for guidance, example, and, above all, sympathy.

CHAPTER III

BACKGROUND AND ATMOSPHERE

THE Turkish home in which I am staying at present has little in common with the harem described by most Western writers, and no doubt those readers accustomed to the *usual* notions of harem life will consider my surroundings disappointingly Western.

Had I been able, as I hoped, to send some photographs of the interior of my friend's house, those photographs would probably be considered " fakes," or perhaps even they might be returned (as they were returned to me when I last stayed in Turkey five years ago) with the comment, " This is not a Turkish harem."

For a long time now, European furniture has been the fashion in Turkish homes. At first this craze for everything Western began in the homes of the Government officials, but it has been gradually spreading ever since, so that to-day, in the smaller homes, cheap, gaudy furniture of the worst kind has replaced the beautiful embroideries and accoutrements of the East. And now the pendulum will swing the other way. With this

new movement of " Turkey for the Turks,"
thinking women like my hostess, who look round
their houses to-day, must necessarily ask themselves the question, " Is this really a Turkish
home ? " With as much zeal, then, as she showed
in filling her house with the ornaments of the lands
she longs to visit, my friend Fâtima has now
begun to collect the furniture, ornaments, and embroideries for the real Turkish room which is to
be mine when next I visit this country. Day after
day we have sauntered through the old bazaar,
which is always an attraction for a woman of the
West, buying those quaint and delightful souvenirs
of the Turkey of the past, in much the same way
as we English who can afford it indulge our tastes
for the furniture and porcelain of a century that is
gone. And when we visit the mosques, too, and
the sacred tombs, we generally come away with
ideas for " my Turkish room," so that next time
I come to Turkey I shall not have the disappointment of travelling all these miles to sleep in a
room furnished with an Empire suite (however
beautiful it may be), a Western sofa, armchairs,
and tables.

Sometimes in the morning when I wake I still
wonder where I really am. Am I in Europe, or
am I in Asia ? My room is as large as any of
the largest rooms in our country houses at home,
and its ceiling and high walls are painted with the
primitive gaudy colouring seen in the mosques.
Fortunately there are seven windows, for there is

no open fireplace, and the room is carpeted from
end to end. A solid silver basin and jug of the
real Eastern shape are on my washstand, the rest
of the toilet service is French, and there is a
Venetian glass bon-bon service, with sweets,
liqueurs, and other drinks, beside my bed, and
tables—tables of all nations. One table put there
specially for my use was a gift from the late Pope
Leo XIII. to my friend's father, and on it stands
a Bible which my friend, though a Moslem, often
reads. On another table stands a signed portrait
of Great Britain's King and Queen, removed for
a short while from its place of honour in the big
salon as a sign of my friend's great affection for
one of their Majesties' humble subjects. It was a
most delightful and delicately turned compliment.
But there are pictures in my room, too, pictures
in a Moslem house! A print water-colour of
Windsor Castle and copies of two of Reynolds's
pictures in the National Gallery, and many English books. Is it surprising that when I look round
this curious room I wonder whether I really am in
Turkey ?

The more I stay in Turkey the more I admire
the inborn aristocracy of the Turk, and yet
" aristocracy " as we understand it does not
exist. Turkey is the country where brotherhood
and equality have been best understood. The
Turkish woman does not often open the doors of
her home to the foreigner, not for lack of any
friendly feeling towards her, but because the

foreigner has lost her confidence, the foreigner has made fun of her, and, above all, the foreigner " pities " her. But when the Turkish woman opens her door to the foreigner, she opens her big, generous heart. Always, however intimate may be their conversations, the honoured guest stands on a pedestal, and the hostess is at her feet longing only for an opportunity of showing courtesy and kindness In no other land have I met with such lavish hospitality—hospitality even that makes one feel a little uncomfortable, especially when one realizes how little one has done to deserve it. The courtesy, also, is almost overwhelming. Every time I go in and out of the room the assembled company, men and women, stand, and every time coffee, cigarettes, and sweets are brought by the slaves for the guests, my hostess rises to serve me herself. Always, too, I sit in the place of honour, as far away from the door as possible, and sometimes right in the draught of the window !

It is the custom, too, for the master of the house to pay all the visitor's bills. That I should have proposed to stamp my own letters hurt my friend. The result is that, nowadays, I write no letters and buy practically nothing. I feel almost guilty when I accept what I do and give nothing in return, and always I have before me the haunting fear of the terrible disappointment my friend will have when she visits my country, for our hospitality cannot be compared to this.

When I asked my friend how long she expected
me to stay, she was surprised at my question.
" As long as ever you like ; you need never go
away ; how I wish you would stay always." And
so it is in most Turkish houses. There are guests
here who came, as I did, for a few days, but they
have never gone away at all ; some even came to
visit Fâtima's grandfather, and still they remain;
they have become part of the house itself.

Fâtima has put her entire trousseau at my dis-
posal. Many of the stuffs and embroideries were
brought to her when she was a child by her
father's friends. They made a special pilgrimage
from the depths of Asia Minor to bring their
offerings to the daughter of the "father of the
people," as the ex-Pasha was known for many
years. I take out these precious gifts sometimes
and examine them at leisure, trying to imagine
the arrival of the "wise men" of the East to
pay honour to the father of the little baby girl
lying in the cradle. For these pilgrims were,
many of them, real "wise men" of the East, and
they brought, amongst other garments, a coat I
am to wear when I dine with European friends,
but I am sure to tremble all the evening for
its safety. The tissue itself is pale blue silk,
the yoke, collar, and cuffs all studded with precious
stones. It is a present from Mecca, and it lies
with the other priceless possessions in my room—
jewels, linen, embroideries, money, and letters
too, in drawers that have no locks, and in a house

where all day long the doors are left open for any to enter who will. Truly, this is a restful civilization!

It was nine o'clock this morning before I tinkled the little silver bell beside my bedstead to summon my " chocolate" attendant. This is a very old Turkish house, and in spite of its Western furniture it rejoices in neither electric bells nor electric light. As a rule, however, my negress is in my room, patiently waiting till I wake, not daring, although she has been asked to do so, to disturb my sleep. Miss Chocolate, clad in a scarlet-coloured dress, her woolly head tied up with a scarlet scarf, brings in two silver trays, on which my breakfast is served. Her skin is like brown velvet. Round her neck she wears a gold necklace, and on her arms she has clanging bangles, which announce her arrival. On one tray Miss Chocolate has collected all kinds of jams, varying from quince to strawberry and violet, and many kinds of biscuits; on the other there are Turkish coffee, milk, powdered chocolate, and tea. Fâtima is generally present to see that I do honour to this curious repast.

My breakfast finished, I follow Miss Chocolate into the marble bath-room attached to my bed-room. But it is not a bath-room which is in the least designed to accompany the Empire suite in my room. A real Eastern bath-room it is, *i.e.* it has a marble floor with a gutter, so that all the water thrown over me runs away, and it contains also the marble basin like a fountain in which the Turks wash, always in running water. The morning after my arrival here I took advantage of Miss Chocolate's leaving me alone for a few minutes to plug up the marble basin, and began to wash as we wash in Europe. But Miss Chocolate returned sooner than I expected, and with much the same expression as the mother who scolds a child who has been playing in the mud, she extracted the handkerchief which served as my plug. "Ach, mattemoiselle," she exclaimed, in Turkish. "What a horrid way to wash!" And she is astonished to see my skin so white— now she knows I have washed all my life in dirtied water. Also when, after meal-time, she pours the water over my hands, she carries away first the basin of dirty water, and then comes back to fetch the jug, thinking it wiser no doubt to keep temptation out of my way.

But not only Miss Chocolate, most of the Turkish women I have met dislike our manner of washing. Indeed, they consider it dangerous to sit in a bath which is not exclusively reserved for their own use. Were they only in other ways to show this fear of spreading disease! But cleanliness, as every one knows, is godliness itself in the Moslem religion, and no doubt the Eastern bath-room will exist even after the veil has disappeared.

Miss Chocolate interests me. She certainly is an excellent maid. She sews well, keeps my clothes well brushed and tidy, washes me well, and has an unending capacity for taking pains. By degrees I shall find out her life history, as I shall find out, perhaps, before I go, the names and social status of all these women here, but I have to work slowly and carefully, lest my sympathetic interest should be mistaken for idle curiosity, and so far I have found out little about my faithful negress. Bought at the age of four by the Pasha, Fâtima's father, for the sum of forty Turkish pounds, she has a record of twenty-five years' faithful servitude. But that is all I know. Since the Constitution, the sale of slaves and eunuchs has been forbidden, and all those at present employed in the house have been offered their liberty. Every slave in this household has, however, refused her liberty, preferring to keep to the original terms of her contract—her freedom only on marriage, with a dowry from the Pasha. Slavery, then, can be considered as no longer existing, and only a few eunuchs remain in the palaces to remind us of an ugly chapter of history that is closed.

Miss Chocolate's features show that she must first have seen the daylight somewhere in the neighbourhood of Lake Tchad. Many lies have been told about the treatment of these slaves, but Miss Chocolate has never been beaten, she receives only kindness; she is invited, with all the other members of the " domestic sisterhood," to see us dance and hear the Western music when we dance and sing in the evenings, but generally we read and sew. And yet never does she nor any other slave take advantage of her mistress's familiarity, standing always at the door, although bidden to come in. And she has a heart of gold. When she saw my face so covered with mosquito bites that I was unfit almost to look upon, the tears ran down her brown cheeks. "And to think," she said, as she rubbed in the ointment, " they might have eaten the whole of my face and it would not have mattered "—the mosquitoes evidently preferred mine.

Before I leave this house I hope to get some photos of the interesting persons it contains, but in undertaking to photograph a Turkish household, I had forgotten first that the windows are dimmed by the inevitable lattice-work, which prevents my having a full view of the wonderful landscape which stretches from the foot of our garden to the rising and setting sun, and when the sun shines it shines through the lattices, throwing on to the furniture all around large lozenge-shaped reflections. But there is another and a greater difficulty, and that is, photography is forbidden by the Moslem religion. My friend would certainly let me photograph the house if I asked her. The sacred law of hospitality is part of her religion. She urged me even to eat bacon in the morning, although pork is forbidden in an Eastern house, and no doubt she would have insisted on buying it had I not declared that even

in my own country I never eat pork. But Fâtima
has to deal with a most fanatical entourage, the
women much more than the men, women who for
centuries have been taught to interpret the Koran
as Mahomet never intended it should be interpreted, women who are purblind to any form of
progress, women who still consider that to reproduce the human form created by God involves
disobedience to the laws of the Prophet, though
the Koran distinctly orders the faithful to march
on with the centuries.

It is extraordinary and interesting to watch the
working of this household.   My host, an exceedingly well-read, intelligent officer, speaking two
European languages, and having served three
years in the German army, is a man with ideas
of feminism and government and social questions
quite half a century before his time, and he is
surrounded by a household of ignorant fanatics
who can neither read nor write.   He would give
his wife complete liberty this very day if it were
possible, and, although she has more liberty than
any woman I know, for her sake he cannot too
openly defy Islam.   The other day one of his
brother officers lunched with us in the harem, but
we were served by the male servants, as every
woman slave refused to appear with bare face
before a man who was not a " blood relation " of
the lady of the house.

There are some ladies here who blame the
Turkish women for not taking their freedom as

other women have done ; there are times, too,
when I feel inclined to sigh for the militant spirit
of the Englishwoman, but until one has really
been behind the veil one can have no idea of
what "fanaticism" really means. Isolated rebellion is of no use—a protest here and there may,
or may not, help, but a movement only really
counts when women march out in an army, and
nothing will ever make them turn back, and there
is no fear of death.

The day I first visited my friend Zeyneb in the
Turkish home which she left six years ago, and
to which she has now returned, the sight of me
in a hat made her forget her surroundings, and,
as she always did in Paris, she eagerly seized my
new hat and tried it on. But she had not counted
with the picturesque old lady seated cross-legged
in the corner of the room alternately smoking and
embroidering. The old lady wore a red tunic
and green pantaloons ; her tobacco and matches
she kept under the arm-chair near which she
worked. She, too, had come on a visit to
Zeyneb's grandmother, and never gone away
again. Perfectly contented with her lot, as are
the women of the last generation, she saw no
reason why the children of this generation should
sigh for a horizon that goes beyond embroidery,
cigarettes, and sweetmeats, especially when it
brings them to forget the sacred commands of the
Prophet. The old lady, at the sight of my
heathenish hat on Zeyneb's head, muttered some-

thing about the giaour I could not understand,
ground her teeth (she is eighty, and still has her
teeth), and cast at both of us a look of the most
profound contempt.   Then it was I first understood what the women of this country must put
up with whenever they try to take a step forward.

"And supposing you were to go into the street
with that hat, what would happen?" I asked
Zeyneb.

"The old lady would rouse the neighbourhood,
we should be seized by an angry mob, and
trampled to death. . . ." I made no comment.
It is not for me to criticize the methods of the
women who are working for liberty.   "These
old women are not immortal," I am assured; "we
are concentrating all our efforts on the future
generation and educating the people.   The rest
will come by itself."

The women are fortunate, however, in having
the Government on their side, and without exag-
geration I may say they have with them most of
the men who count at all, for what thinking man
could see any chance of progress while this
absurd separation of the sexes continues?   I
don't say the Turk wants for his womenkind the
liberty of the English or American women.   He
does not even want them to work, but he does
want them, for his sake, to take part in the social
life going on around them.   The Turk likes
society, and he likes theatres, but to-day, unless
he has married a Christian woman, he must go

there by himself, borrow some one else's wife, or stay at home.

" Why should I go out and amuse other people's wives and leave my own wife at home ? " said my host one day ; and very rarely does he go out in the evening ; but all Turks are not like my host. The Minister of the Interior, Talaat Bey, a man of surprising energy, with a clear understanding of men and things, a real God-send to this country in its present state, encourages any work for the advancement of women, and he is paying particular attention to their education. The military governor of Constantinople, Djémal Bey, too, has given instructions that the liberty of the women is not to be interfered with, and no doubt in time his word will become law.

The women, however, as I said before, have made enormous progress in five years. What would have happened five years ago if Fâtima and I had driven home from a family party with her husband at the " indecent " hour of 9.30 ? Five years ago we never walked a step ; now we not only saunter through the bazaar, but go to a big dressmaker's in Pera, whilst formerly all our goods had to be purchased from Greek merchants and Paris dressmakers who came with their goods to the harem. But not only in the bazaar do we walk ; we have walked in the magnificent newly laid-out park, where women are allowed for the first time to walk, in a park where there are men. The men, I must say, have not yet grown accustomed to this new and extraordinary state of things, and vie with the Levantine " mashers " in their desire to see the features under the veil.   It is not a very comfortable experience for the Turkish women, but it is the darkness before the dawn.   The dawn is coming slowly ; but it will come if the Turkish woman really wishes it, and works always with that aim before her—the uplifting of her sex.

CHAPTER IV

THE IMPERIAL HAREM—A RECEPTION
BY THE SULTAN

IT has been the privilege of many foreigners
visiting Constantinople to witness the ceremony
of *baise-main*, which takes place at the Dolma
Bagtché Palace, but it does not fall to the lot of
every woman to see that imposing ceremony from
the Imperial harem. This unique and interesting
experience I owe to my hostess, Fâtima.

The ceremony of baise-main is too well known
for me to describe it here, and those persons who
were seated in the gallery reserved for the Corps
Diplomatique would no doubt see to better
advantage than I the throne-room, the Sultan,
and the curious and many-coloured uniforms and
costumes of the Ottoman subjects who paid their
homage to the Kaliph of Islam. Through the
lattice-work windows of the Imperial harem it
was difficult to form more than a vague idea of
the ceremony, for we were so many women
huddled together on the cushions, so many who
were trying to see, that after a few moments I
gave my seat to another lady in order to wander

3   33

at leisure through the Imperial harem, where
Fâtima tells me I am the first Englishwoman to
be admitted as a visitor.

It was the first day of Baïram. We were
awakened at dawn by the plaintive cries of the
sacrificed sheep. Réchad, the coachman, was
chosen as vékil (sacrificer), because he is recognized by the whole household as the most pious
of us all, and his forty-five years of service also
demand that this privilege should be his. His,
too, was the privilege of distributing the meat,
the skin, and the horns of the four sheep which
this Moslem household offered to the poor, who
came in through the open gates like a pack of
hungry wolves, and looked, with their poor
ravenous eyes, as if they could tear the meat
from the hands of the coachman. To me, standing on the balcony, it was like watching a scene
from the Old Testament—a scene all out of focus
with so many of the attempts at progress which
I see around this beautiful and interesting capital.

How strange it seemed also to be dressing for
Court at 6.30 in the morning! To be putting
on thin silk evening dresses and slippers at
that early hour, and driving away in the chilly
morning to pay our homage to an Eastern
monarch.

Fâtima's dress was of pink crêpe-de-chine
embroidered in dull silver—a Paris creation—
the last, however, she will ever have embroidered outside Turkey, for, like so many other

ladies here, she has now awakened to the fact that the most costly embroideries of Europe are but poor imitations of the work of her own land. Round her hair she wore a pink and silver scarf, attached to the side by a silver rose, a charming variation of the curious turbans of flowers, feathers, and jewels which are worn by so many of the ladies attending the Ottoman Court. I asked Fâtima if the Court officials gave instructions to the ladies regarding their dress. " Provided their hair be decently covered," she replied, " etiquette is satisfied," and the Caliph has the " supreme" privilege of seeing all his subjects unveiled.

Like most of the ladies of the Court, we were attended by a slave, my negress, Miss Chocolate, an interesting personage in her Court attire. For this occasion she was dressed in pale blue satin, with a pale blue turban trimmed with pink roses, her fingers, arms, and neck being covered not only with all the jewellery she possessed, but the jewellery of the other slaves. It was her duty to follow us all the while, and during luncheon she stood inside the door with folded arms, in case her services should be required. It was she who took charge of our little bags, and in one of the "grandmother" pockets of her wide satin skirt were hair pins, safety pins, and handkerchiefs, in case of emergency. To drive to the Court, Miss Chocolate wore a white tulle veil which entirely covered her face, and a vivid blue satin feridji, covered with sequins and big white velvet pansies. How I wish I could have photographed her! Fâtima wore a yashmak, now, alas! only worn by Princesses and ladies attending the Court, for to me it is one of the most becoming of head-dresses, showing the eyes to very great advantage. She wore, also, a peacock-blue satin feridji, a hideous contrast to Miss Chocolate's electric blue.

The Imperial harem, in spite of certain changes and certain privileges accorded to the Imperial Ottoman Princes and Princesses, still remains the harem in the real sense of the word, the harem about which Western readers expect to hear, the part of the Oriental house exclusively reserved for the use of the women. Across its threshold no man may enter, and even as we drove into the big door, which is inside another wooden door, and which is opened to admit each carriage and shut again immediately, our footman had to descend and wait for us outside the door. The whole Imperial harem is surrounded by a wall so high that no passer-by can possibly see within. The coachman, too, having left us at the entrance door, had to drive out and wait outside the first door.

This is the first time since I have been back again in Turkey that I have felt myself really within a harem. Even when I wear a veil, even when I forget I am not in England and try to push back the fixed lattice windows, even when

I take part in these Baïram dinners, where not even the master of the house may be present, I do not realize the atmosphere of the harem. But within the palace, amidst its curious assembly of slaves and eunuchs, and in spite of its wide corridors and immense salons, there is a most uncomfortable feeling of bondage which would turn me into a raving lunatic at the end of a week. It is true, Fâtima explains to me, that all these women are solemnly asked four times at the end of each year whether they would like to marry and leave the harem. I say to myself, then, if they stay it is because they wish to stay, and are therefore happy. Their existence, however, seems a most heartrending waste of human life, and as I sat watching them loitering along the exquisitely carpeted corridors, gossiping, smoking, carrying alternately coffee and water to the guests, I longed to break down for them the lattice-work which always is there between them and the sun, to fling the windows wide open, so that they could breathe in the fresh air, and open the doors so that they, too, might go out. And yet not one of these women seemed in the least to feel her slavery, and, no doubt, they would turn their backs in horror on the ugly, unprotected existence of some of the women of my country.

" But these slaves are perfectly happy," again and again Fâtima assured me, and, to judge from their smiling faces, I suppose they are. But

waste is always sad—waste of youth, waste of
beauty, waste of womanhood, especially when
women are so sorely needed for the regeneration
of this country.

Arrived at the central entrance door of the
harem, Fâtima and I were helped out of our
carriage by the attendant eunuchs. I was told
that eunuchs were now a thing of the past, but
certainly that remark could not have been made
with reference to the Imperial harem.   It is
difficult for me, however, to remember that these
poor mutilated anachronisms are great personages
at the Ottoman Court, who, although they perform the menial service of opening the carriage
doors and helping us up the stairs (one on either
side and one behind, as though we were old
ladies), are yet the masters of the establishment.
Fâtima explained to me that they spoke to her
with the exaggerated politeness of the Eastern
courtier, because of their affection for her father,
and all of them came to ask for news of him.

At the first turning of the central staircase we
walked into the yashmak room, where a host of
female slaves came forward to help us. I felt
for a moment as though I had strayed behind
the scenes at Drury Lane, so curious they
looked, in their brightly coloured figured silks
and clashing coloured turbans, but their dyed
hair and blackened eyes should be my excuse
for the poor compliment I am paying them.
Some of the costumes, it is true, were made of

those priceless Persian embroideries for which
Fâtima and I have searched the market-place,
but always the *tout ensemble* was spoilt by some
vividly coloured and clashing turban, a vivid
yellow dress with a bright pink head-dress, an
electric-blue dress and an exaggeratedly blue
turban, which made one's eyes ache. Behind
the footlights, perhaps, such combinations could
pass muster, but in the daylight, even in the
dim daylight which comes through the latticed
windows, they were a motley, uncomfortable
spectacle. These dresses, however, defied both
time and fashion, and were all cut on the same
model ; a long dress, with the train caught up to
the waist, and a sack jacket.

Once the yashmak and our cloaks were removed
the slaves took away the veils to iron them, and
other slaves arrived to conduct us upstairs and
announce our arrival to the lady Court officials,
who wore costumes of different colours according
to their rank. There was, first of all, the
Hasnadar Ousta, or High Controller of the
establishment, in white satin, trimmed with real
gold embroidery at the foot of her dress and at
the bottom of her coat. Her little white and gold
turban suited her perfectly, and her jewels, if not
beautiful, at least were original. On her breast
was a bouquet of diamond flowers, which stretched
almost from shoulder to shoulder. Another
diamond ornament stretched across the front of
her turban, and in her ears she wore birds the

size of butterflies, each holding in its mouth a
pearl the size of a cherry. She was an old
lady, judging by her wrinkled face and bent
back, rather than her golden hair, and after she
had walked once or twice round the assembled
ladies, kissing some and saluting others, leaning
on her stick of office, she hobbled into the
presence of one of the Princesses, leaving the
real duties of the day to the younger officials.

I would have liked to ask one of the Court
officials, had I dared, how our dresses appeared
to them. The wife of the War Minister was
wearing a dress of cerise *crêpe-de-chine*, so tight
that she had to sit down carefully. All the
ladies wore silk stockings and high-heeled shoes
—most of them might have come straight out
of the paper *Chiffons* which is carefully studied
in up-to-date harems to-day. How strange
we all must have looked to these uncorseted
women, who made no attempt at a fashionable
coiffure, who still remained faithful to the
" babouches " (heelless slippers) and coloured
stockings worked with gold, and whose dresses
could have been made into three or four of our
present-day creations.

Most of the Court officials wore the Grand
Cordon of the Order of the Chefakat, the Order
of Mercy given to ladies of high rank and distinguished lady visitors. Fâtima alone amongst
the lady visitors wore that order. Every time
the Court officials passed, the guests stood, as

the Eastern etiquette demands they should in the presence of superiors and aged ladies. This, however, was rather uncomfortable for us, for the Assistant Treasurer had known Fâtima's family all her life, and frequently came and spoke to us. Seeing us about to rise, with Eastern politeness she ordered us to remain seated, but Eastern politeness also demanded that we should disregard her request and rise to speak to her.

The Assistant Hasnadar was particularly interested in me when, after much beating about the bush, Fâtima at last owned that I had never had a husband. "We are companions in distress," said the Hasnadar, which in her case was not true, as I have already explained. A husband would be found for her to-morrow if she wished. But the wherefore of my celibacy puzzled her. "It is nothing of which to be ashamed," I protested. "It is nothing of which to be proud," she answered, and, like an Eastern woman when unable to reply, I shrugged my shoulders and laughed. The joys of "single blessedness" are not understood in this country, and personally, outside these high Court officials, I have never met an old Turkish spinster.

But supposing any of these women should take advantage of the solemn asking once a year, whether or no they will marry, what becomes of them? We have at present living in our harem a slave who has just left one of the Princess's palaces. Fâtima has undertaken to

keep her here until she and her friends can find
a suitable husband for her. She is a contented, beautiful, useless creature, who eats with
us when the young Bey is not here, and sings
Oriental songs of exquisite pathos, accompanying
herself on the oude.[1]   And sometimes, when she
sings, I ask Fâtima to interpret the words of them.
" It is an old, old Turkish love-song," she said,
"a beautiful old song, and I love to hear her
sing it."   " And what kind of love-song does a
Turkish man sing to his unknown bride?" I asked.
" That all the sorrows in the world may be his
lot, if only all the joys may be hers."   " And what
is the most awful of all the sorrows?" I asked.
" Solitude," answers Fâtima without hesitation.

We were a curious luncheon party that day—
the wife of the Sultan's Master of Ceremonies,
several of Fâtima's friends, and an Egyptian
Princess, whose arrival at the Palace in a magnificent steam launch I had seen through the harem
lattices.   Most of these ladies, who spoke quite
fluent French, were too timid to speak to me,
a most distressing modesty, especially when it
necessitates the constant employment of Fâtima
as interpreter.   If only they could hear how
unmercifully most of us Englishwomen handle
foreign languages, whilst they are really excellent
linguists (the best in Europe, except, perhaps,
the Russians), they surely would take courage.

The meal the Sultan offered us could scarcely

---

[1] Oude : Turkish guitar played with a feather.

be called a luncheon. There were cold meats of various kinds, sweatmeats, creams, and other delicacies, served in Sèvres dishes, but water was the only beverage. And after the meal was over, the slaves came round offering us glasses of water in beautifully cut crystal goblets, with gold lids, and served on little golden dishes. It was extraordinary to me to be bidden to an Emperor's feast and given only water to drink, and yet here water is so limpid and cold that it is often more acceptable than the best champagne, and often on the steamboat, when we travel, I call the water-seller, who frequently passes in and out of the harem part of the boat in which we travel, and purchase a penny glass of water.

The ceremony of baise-main in the Selamlik was finished about eleven. To the cry of " Oh, Sultan, be humble, and remember God is greater than you," from the assembled Court, the Sultan retired for a short rest before coming to the harem to receive the ladies of the Court. And, perhaps, he slept longer that day than he intended, for it seemed to us an eternity to wait. Eight hours at a Court, however, would be considered tiring in most countries, but most particularly in a harem where male conversation cannot be procured for untold gold. I begin to miss the society of the opposite sex: it is true we have men, far more men, in our Turkish home than in any other Turkish home I know, but I miss the men at the parties and picnics and meetings. And it does seem rather a waste of time to put on my prettiest gowns and make a particularly handsome coiffure to eat only with women. Zeyneb used to say that " men spoiled the look of our Western functions; that they crawled about our drawing-rooms and ball-rooms like great black-beetles." Surely she had forgotten the appearance of an Ottoman Court and the awful black-beetles that crawl about there, when she spoke so disparagingly of our Western assemblies.

Fâtima explained to me that the Court of the present Sultan in no way equals the Court of the ex-Sultan in magnificence. The embroidery which the slaves hold in front of the coffee tray whilst coffee is being served was only a plain gold embroidery, whilst in Abdul Hamid's time the cloth was studded with real stones. The coffee cups, too, and the jam service were only solid gold, whilst in Abdul Hamid's time jewelled coffee cups were always used. The Court, how-ever, has become more democratic. Princesses walk about amongst the people as they were not allowed to do during the reign of Abdul Hamid, and but for their red enamel necklaces and large diamond orders, exclusively worn by members of the Imperial family, we should have scarcely known we were amongst the members of the Imperial family. The Sultan's grand-daughter interested me particularly—not so much because of her rank, but because of her appearance. She is a short girl for her age, which, I believe, is about twelve, but her dress was long and wide, her hair dressed in a knot on the top of her head inside a diamond crown, and the front of her small body was covered with diamond orders and a diamond dog-collar encircled her little throat. But most curious of all was the long, thin hand, quite out of proportion to the size of her body, with which she acknowledged our *temenahs* (Eastern salutations), and on those curious hands she wore gold mittens studded with rubies and diamonds. It looked as though she had utilized a gold purse for that purpose. She had a charming and interesting face, this little Princess, though one of unending sadness. She looked to me not unlike a school-girl acting the part of Queen Elizabeth, and a striking contrast to the merry little Princesses of her age in our Western countries.

But what is most delightful to me in Turkish life, in the Court and out of the Court, in fact in every station of life, is the beautiful feeling of democracy. A Princess, while talking to you, will suddenly excuse herself, rise and throw her arms round the neck of her old *nourrice*, who walks about amongst the highest of the Court ladies. The accident of high birth demands specially cultured conversation, kindness, and fine manners towards persons of humbler birth, argues the Turkish woman, and the *snobbery* which is so frequent in our Western countries has never existed here.

But suddenly one becomes conscious of a certain movement amongst the ladies, who, in spite of the music of the Imperial orchestra playing in the garden of the palace, in spite of the Hasnadar's merry laugh and her encouraging request to be "patient," have been growing weary of waiting. The Sultan has arrived! He has taken a particularly long rest this day, changed the uniform in which he received the Ottoman officials for a simple morning coat, and is seated in an armchair in the big salon waiting the arrival of the ladies in the order which the Hasnadar should see fit to introduce them. A procession of four ladies at a time, headed by the Hasnadar, we enter the room where Mehmeth V. is seated. But it is a ceremony so intimate, so unlike the ceremony we had dimly seen a few hours before through the latticed windows, that I cannot bring myself to think this good-natured, unceremonious old gentleman is the Sultan of a great Empire.

To me, we had the appearance of four students going to an examination, and I felt this more when, after kneeling before the Caliph, as etiquette demands, and kissing his hand, we were requested to rise and be introduced. "Your Majesty, our Sultan, Commander of the Faithful," began the Hasnadar, with bent head, and leaning on her stick of office, " this is the

daughter of —— and the wife of —— " Then the
Sovereign Caliph congratulated her on being the
daughter of —— and the wife of ——, said he was
delighted to make her acquaintance, and passed
on to the next lady, who was introduced in the
same manner.   When Fâtima's name was made
known to his Majesty, he asked her to be seated,
and, again kneeling before the Sultan, she gave
him news of her father, and answered the many
questions he asked.

This was the first time Fâtima had made the
acquaintance of the Sultan.   " He was delighted,"
he said with Eastern courtesy, and Fâtima rose
and asked permission to introduce me herself.
I was not introduced as the daughter or wife of a
well-known Pasha, but as Fâtima's " English
sister," who had come to share her existence for
a while, and who had now come with her to pay
homage to the Sovereign of the country.   Many
questions the Sultan asked about me, about my
country, and all the while he talked I was
thinking of the poor captive, Prince Réchad, who
for thirty-three years had been imprisoned
within those walls, and who now was the Sultan
seated before me.   He was weary.   Early rising,
perhaps, suited him as little as it suited me.   He
frequently pulled himself up, forced his eyes open,
said he was delighted to make our acquaintance.
Then we rose, and the Hasnadar escorted us from
the room, and on the same occasion four more
Court ladies were led into the Imperial presence.

It is interesting naturally to meet the ruler of a
country, of an empire of such tradition, of a land
which will be for so many years to come the
subject of the greatest interest, but the meeting
of the present Sultan did not stir me as did the
meeting of the ex-Sultan Abdul Hamid—Abdul
Hamid, who pretended not to know one word of
the French language, which he speaks fluently,
who always played his part, and took particular
care that part should be well played before
foreigners. All the nicest-sounding words were
chosen from the Turkish language to delight
their ears. He humbly requested that the
distinguished foreigner for a short while staying
within the capital of his " dear " land would make
known to him the manner in which the Government could be of service in helping the foreigner
on his or her journey. His great, big, brown
eagle eyes were wide awake, he *unpacked* the
distinguished visitor, whilst the interpreter
translated into the language he knows so well,
and this hideous tyrant became a being of fas-
cination. The present Sultan is a " fatalist."
Could he be otherwise with such an agonizing
past? He who was obedient to his brother is
now obedient to the Constitution ; perhaps for
Turkey it is better he should be so.

.   .   .   .   .

We drove home in silence, Fâtima and I. She
had explained so many things to me that day ;
now she was tired. A long, tiring, but interest-

ing day it was. I was almost sorry it had to end. Miss Chocolate, in her gaudy attire, is sitting in front of us in the carriage, weeping at the honour conferred on her, for she, with all the other slaves, has kissed the ground on which the master's feet were resting. . . . Cannon are firing to announce that the time for evening prayer has come ; the fat, unexercised horses are ploughing their way up the hill ; the shops, which at 4.30 are pulling down their shutters for the night as we drive by, have had a day of rest. . . . What a wonderful change it is to be a Turkish woman for a while. . . . Surely Fate was kind to me when she crossed my destiny with that of little Fâtima.

CHAPTER V

THE ANGEL OF DEATH

THE Baïram festivities have ended sorrowfully for us. This house, which a few days ago echoed with mirth and laughter, is now silent— as silent as a grave. The whole Konak is as if it were covered with a pall of ice ; the happy faces of the slaves have now an expression of woe ; the long stream of ladies who came to visit us at Baïram have returned to mingle their sorrows with ours—the beloved master of this house is dead. He was spending the winter in Cyprus ; his Baïram telegram said he was in perfect health : but even before the news reached us he was sleeping beside his father in the little cemetery by the sea, buried within twenty-four hours of his death, as is the custom here ; and the grand old man of Turkey was laid to rest like the most humble of the Sultan's subjects.

We Westerners, with our curious ideas of Eastern life, cannot imagine the picturesque, simple, and natural attitude the Turks have towards death. None of the hideous wailing, the rending of garments, sackcloth and ashes (supposed to be part of the Eastern mourning) ; none of our Western terrifying preparation for the long last journey ; no mourning, no flowers, no funeral cards ; it is as if the dear one had gone on a journey to a foreign land, and his family and friends pray for him as if he were still alive. A Turkish burial, however, is impressive in its simplicity. A plain wooden coffin, covered with a Persian shawl, and a fez at its head, is carried on the shoulders of the relatives and friends.

When the dead man's eyes are closed the Hodja is called, and he reads for the comfort of the bereaved ones some verses of the Koran. Then he pauses, and solemnly asks those persons present whether they consider their relative an upright, honourable man—a curious custom, this seems to me ; it is almost as if the Hodja were preparing for the dead man a passport for the next world. (I write these words with all reverence.) It is not always, however, that the assembled mourners answer the Hodja's question in the affirmative. If their conscience tells them to speak the truth they do so, and the Hodja answers simply, " Then forgive your brother his sins, as Allah will forgive you," and the assembled mourners pass on to the grave.

To me it has seemed a little strange to see the sons of wealthy Pashas buried as only the poor in our country world be buried. When I questioned a friend about this she answered, " The money you people in the West spend on funeral pomp we

give to the poor assembled round the grave, and
according to the deceased's years and fortune.
Supposing a rich man of 83 is buried, eighty-three
sovereigns would be distributed amongst the poor ;
when a man of 83 and of moderate means, eighty-
three francs, or even eighty-three pence, as the
case may be. The poor are never forgotten in
this country ; they come to the marriage feast,
they come to the Baıram festivities, every day
they come to this house and are fed, and even
during death they are not neglected."

We, the women of the house, do not follow
the coffin to the grave. Twice since my short
stay here the Angel of Death has visited this
house. The Pasha's grandson left us first of all,
and now the Pasha himself is " not here," which
is my Turkish friend's expression to avoid pro-
nouncing the word " death."

For days now, streams of visitors have come
to show their sympathy. The door leading to
the *selamlik* has been left open for all the men
friends who will to enter, and the door leading
to the *haremlik* has been left open for any women
who care to enter. But what a curious assembly
of visitors ! What a lesson in " equality " ! Some
of the callers were the wives of Ministers of State,
some were the wives and daughters of generals,
admirals, and the most honoured of Turkey's
great men, some were almost beggars, but they
were all together in the same room. Death, the
great leveller, had brought them together to mourn

the loss of a personal friend, and we of the household were grateful for the sympathy of them all.

According to their custom, the ladies made their *temenahs* (Eastern salutations) to the hostess, which she acknowledged, rising, however, to kiss the hand of the old ladies, some of whom came from long distances to take part in the mourning. They came in bright colours many of these callers, which seemed strange to me, accustomed from my birth to the habit of outward mourning.

When the visitors have taken their seats, they make their *temenahs* to all the assembled guests, and the guests acknowledge their salutations; it is a picturesque manner of saying "How do you do?" When first I arrived here I frequently forgot to acknowledge the *temenahs* of the guests. A veil, after all, does not make a Turkish woman. My thoughts at the time were far away, but the look of surprise at my lack of breeding called me to order, and I pay particular attention now to what are elementary points in good education.

Whilst sipping my coffee, as very few of the ladies speak, or, if they speak, they do so in a whisper, I carefully study the assembled guests. The wife of —— Pasha is wearing a bright blue satin dress and *tcharchaff* (Turkish cape and veil), high-heeled shoes, and open-worked silk stockings; a scarf of ermine is round her neck. At her feet, sitting cross-legged on the floor, is an ex-slave dealer, a woman in a tattered red

tcharchaff. She has left her shoes outside.
Near her are a bath attendant and a poor woman,
who usually sits nursing her miserable offspring
not far from our gate; they sit silently weeping,
these women, for the benefactor who is no more,
and without uttering one word they rise, politely
bow to the assembled guests, put on their shoes,
and disappear through the open door of the
harem.

Every time coffee is served—and coffee is
offered to every visitor—I take a cup; it gives
me a better chance of studying the curious scene
in which I am playing a part, and the more I
look, the more beautiful it seems to me, and it
makes me almost sad to think I cannot meet
this spirit of democracy in any other land. But
the most beautiful part of it all is the absolute "naturalness" of the situation. The rich
woman has not the patronizing attitude of the
Western woman towards her humbler sisters,
the poor woman has not the cringing gratitude
of the West for favours received; each knows
her part—the woman whose birth and education
entitle her to a chair and the woman whose
education teaches her, her place is on the floor,
and who, even though the high-born woman
invites her to sit on a chair, refuses. Each is
fulfilling her destiny—each is content with her
lot.

I do not swear by everything Turkish, much
as I love the Turks. They have their faults;

which nation has not its faults? but, as a woman
who has led the life of a Turkish woman, surely
I am privileged to point out to the reader the
most beautiful features of this life as I see them.
We have been unjust to Turkey; we have for
so long confounded the Turkish subjects with
the cruel despots of the Hamidian régime; we
have for so long now condemned wholesale everything Turkish, and the novel-writers of the day
describe a Turkey which certainly does not exist
to-day.

I have so often explained the meaning of the
word harem; the papers have repeated my explanation; but I still receive letters asking the
most primitive questions I would be ashamed
to repeat to my friends. They who know our
history and literature as few in England know
it, how would they feel were they to have an
idea of what Europe thought of them? How
is it possible for a British official, after long
residence here, to ask whether we eat with our
fingers? How could a man of any intelligence
suppose that my host, who has eaten at the
Kaiser's table, could come back to his own
country and eat with his fingers? One feels
inclined to treat the question with the contempt
one feels for the questioner, but silence is consent,
and one of the reasons why the modern Turk
is so misjudged to-day is because he has treated
these calumnies with silent contempt.

To the British official I answer, then, we eat

with Sheffield knives and forks, we eat off British
plates, we sit on British chairs, we have a
British table, British linen, and a British side-
board, and in every corner of this house is some
token of the very great love the late Pasha had
for my country.

And the word harem! When will Europe
understand the meaning of that unfortunate
word? An Arabic word, meaning "sacred" or
"forbidden," it is used to describe those rooms
in a Turkish house exclusively reserved for
the women. Imagine for a moment a konak
(Turkish palace, a large Turkish country house),
situated on a hill, and with a magnificent view
over the Sea of Marmora and its picturesque
islands. The wooden gates are always open,
the beggars enter at leisure and loiter in the
carriage-drive, and walk along the garden paths,
and sit under the trees and eat the fruit, so that
unless you notice you have entered a gate you
would imagine yourself still on the road. To
the ordinary tourist this garden would seem a
mass of ruins, a waste heap, a place most shame-
fully neglected. But the connoisseur knows at
once the priceless treasures it contains, relics
of Byzantine fountains, crypts, cornerstones, for
which Western museums would give a fortune.

There are two entrances to this Turkish house.
One leads into the selamlik, and the door leading
into the harem is at the side. In the selamlik,
or men's quarters, there are reception-rooms, a

dining-room, and bed-rooms for the unmarried
male relations living here. A door in the selamlik
leads into a big salon, and a door also from the
harem leads into this same big salon. It is here
that European guests are received, having entered
by the door of the selamlik, and this is all they
see of a Turkish house; it is here they must find
all the material for their romances of Turkish
life. Occasionally through the open door they
catch a glimpse of some of the ladies of the
house who pass by the door, and who strictly
keep their hair veiled. They see, perhaps, the
slaves in their picturesque costumes, and immediately the thought of "polygamy" enters
their mind; all these ladies must be the wives
of the Pasha.

Polygamy does not exist, nowadays, in Turkey,
or at least it is very exceptional. Even many
members of the Imperial family content themselves with one wife. The reason for this is
only too obvious. "When four wives meant to
their possessor four tillers of the land," said a
witty Pasha, the other day, "there was some
sense in polygamy, but not when they buy their
dresses at Paquin's." Setting aside, however,
the economic question, where is the woman to
be found who would tolerate a rival in her own
home, and supposing she did, what kind of a life
would the poor master lead?

A story is told of a pious Moslem who was
always the first in the mosque. "How is it

you are so early?" one day his friend asked
him; "however early I come, you are always
here." "I have two wives," answered the
pious man; "I get away as soon as I possibly
can."

The Turkish woman is proud, and insists that
her dignity be respected, and, personally, I know
few who would put up with the "polygamy"
which women of the Latin races are obliged to
accept. When a Turkish woman marries, her
husband is obliged according to his means to
make a settlement; this sum becomes hers
should she find it necessary to divorce him. So
when a wife has cause for complaint she claims
her dowry and personal effects, and returns to
her family or nearest relative, and both husband
and wife are free to marry again.

Marriages can be made and unmade here with
a rapidity that would astonish even our Trans-
atlantic cousins. Reform of the marriage and
divorce laws is urgently needed, and yet when
you come to look at the question carefully,
regrettable as this easy divorce is, it is astonishing
how few men take advantage of their privilege.
In a country where public opinion considers a
man's private life belongs exclusively to him,
where men and women take their pleasures apart,
where men are so frequently obliged to seek the
society of European women, and divorce is as
easy as saying "Good morning," it seems in-
credible to me that the Turkish households run

along so smoothly. Perhaps it is that the Turkish wife, feeling her insecure position, takes particular care to please her lord and master; perhaps it is that the Turk is, as a rule, a good husband and father; perhaps it is that he sees in his wife a charm the European does not possess. At any rate, to a foreigner these laws appear as though they were made to lead men into temptation.

Many people have stayed to lunch this week, none of them, of course, invited. Always our table is laid for twelve persons, although sometimes we are only three to lunch. Those who call in the morning stay to lunch as a matter of course; the hostess would feel herself slighted were they to go away without sharing her meal. She it is who is under obligations to her guests for honouring her with their presence.

The two principal meals here, lunch and dinner, are unending, and generally extend to twelve or fifteen courses, quite ten of those courses being vegetables cooked in oil or cooked with the meat, and, the goodness of the meat having given itself to the vegetables, it is not served at table, but is given to the beggars or the endless army of cats which inhabits the basement of a Turkish house. These cats, fortunately, understand their place is downstairs unless they are invited upstairs. Stamboul will soon be as overcrowded with cats, as Pera was with dogs. "Why do you not drown some of them?" I asked a member of

this household. " It would be a sin according
to the Koran," said he; "we only kill animals
to eat them."

Turkish cooking, delicious though it be, is not
the diet for most of the ladies here, and certainly
not for me. Cheese *bereks*, of pastry, so thin
that they fall in bits before you can get them
into your mouth. *Kadaif*, biscuits soaked in
treacle and covered with sugared cream, the
breast of chicken ground into a powder and
served with cream and chocolate—I feel I need
four hours' hard riding to digest properly the
dishes the hospitable Turks set before us, and
I have scarcely walked five hundred yards in six
weeks.

This lack of physical exercise and air is to me
one of the most unfortunate features of Turkish
life. It is true the windows are open, but the sun
shining through the lattice windows does not have
a chance of playing its proper part; it can neither
warm the house nor kill the microbes. This
would not matter so much if the ladies spent more
time out of doors, or if, when they are out of
doors, they kept their veils up. There is absolutely no reason now why they should not; the
police have strict orders from the "feminist"
Military Governor of Constantinople to interfere
in no way with the ladies, and any man daring to
insult a woman is punished with exile.

But the slavery of ages cannot be cast aside in
a few months, and the ladies continue to wear

their thick black canvas veils over their faces. Through this veil the beautiful coloured landscape becomes a black-and-white sketch. On hot days it is unbearable; one has a tendency to squint because of looking through the holes in order to see, and it makes one's eyes ache if one suddenly throws it back and comes into the full glare of the sunshine. And yet the Turkish woman still wears her veil down. "You see," said Djémal Bey (the Military Governor of Constantinople), "they will not take advantage of the liberty I try to give them."

And now the men, not the women, curious as it may seem to Western minds, have awakened to the fact that this lack of physical exercise is beginning to show most distressing results in the poor anæmic children born of these mothers who take no exercise. Nowadays, when thinking men no longer accept the decrees of the Church as the supreme verdict, but begin to judge for themselves, progress is possible.

Formerly, when the weaklings died off, the faithful bowed their heads in resignation: Kismet, "it is written," said they. Now the indefatigable Minister of the Interior, Talaat Bey, who has ordered fifty schools to be opened during the next year, is importing into the country teachers of Swedish drill. I took part the other day in the first lesson given to the girls. How interesting it was to see their wide-awake, wondering eyes, their look of disgust when the teacher appeared in knickerbockers and unveiled in the presence of the male inspector — they who, though only ten to twelve, had their hair closely veiled. And the mothers who came upon the scene, and with tears in their eyes begged that they might have their children back, for they could not understand what these Western women were doing with them. How strange and curious it all is, this awakening of a people after centuries of sleep !

In this work of regeneration, again, we have not given the Turks either the praise or justice they deserve. It is when one is behind the scenes, and sees the difficulties the Turks have to contend with that one can appreciate their efforts. It is true they have made mistakes ; youth and inexperience always make mistakes— that is the natural order of things. It would certainly have been better for Turkey to have made more mistakes and had the advantage of the lesson those mistakes bring than to have relied on Europe for assistance. The duty of Europe should have been to help the Turks to help themselves, instead of which all along the line they have stepped in and taken the bread from their mouths.

Here are these Turks struggling against the tyranny of a religion which is not the religion of Mahomet ; they are striving for a more intelligent interpretation of the Koran, especially on the subject of women and the veil. The all-powerful

Sheik-ul-Islam, whose followers are principally amongst the turban-headed men in Asia Minor interferes with progress, as the Church always does when Church and State are combined. When Djemil Pasha, the Prefect of Constantinople, opened a beautiful park in Stamboul, and gave men and women permission to walk in that park at the same time, the Sheik-ul-Islam issued a decree forbidding the women to walk in this park the same day as the men. Then Talaat Bey, with a boldness yet unknown in Islam, issued a decree ignoring the Sheik-ul-Islam, and gave women and men permission to walk in the park on the same days.

All these reforms are going on in what Europe considers an almost bankrupt State. Education, new roads, industries, a new navy—everything is needed ; but Turkey will pull herself together if only she has confidence in herself.

CHAPTER VI

CHAMPIONS OF WOMEN—THE MEN
WHO LEAD

I HAVE been to one of the Turkish feminist meetings, which take place every Friday afternoon upon which it is possible to find speakers. This society is not organized according to our Western methods, there being no responsible head and no list of members. It has not even a battle-cry, as, for example, "the vote," nor an official name; it is the society where the different interests of women are discussed, and its best appellation, perhaps, would be "the society for the elevation of womanhood." From articles which have from time to time appeared in our papers I imagined there was in Turkey an organized society for the abolition of the veil, and that "man," the arch-enemy of woman, was the chief obstacle to woman's progress. I believe, however, this idea is prevalent in our Western countries.

Signed always with the name of a Turkish woman, these articles are written by persons who are catering for readers of sensation. The names of the writers are unknown here amongst the feminists, the statements most emphatically denied ; it is not to the women's advantage to be described as these articles describe them—beautiful, idle creatures airing their grievances to the women of the West. A Turkish woman never airs her grievances, most certainly not to foreigners, and those who come into intimate contact with her know she resents being asked questions, and she does not ask to be pitied.

I have pointed out in previous chapters that for the present the Turkish woman's aim is not to cast aside the veil, and also the fact which is still almost incomprehensible to me, viz. the encouragement the men are giving to the women in their work. It is they who are trying to give the women courage ; they who are urging the women to be a little bolder in their tactics, and who, in their writings and speeches, are imploring them to leave no stone unturned to hasten their enfranchisement. I am told that the men have even written articles for the newly founded woman's paper, and signed them with feminine names, for the number of women writers here is still very limited. The cultured women, it is true, speak Turkish, but as their education has been given by French or English governesses, the study of their own language has been neglected, and at present they can best express themselves in a language not their own.

My friends speak and write to one another

5

in French; hence, when Fâtima and I walk,
which is very rarely, and speak to one another in
French, no one supposes that one of these veiled
figures is an Englishwoman. It seems almost to
a stranger that French is the language of the
country, and Turkish is for the poor and unedu-
cated, although the members of the new
Nationalist movement would not be happy to
hear this. They are, however, setting themselves
to the task of learning their own language, which
they have neglected, and many are doing so with a
view to writing. Halidé-Hanoum, the most talented
of Turkish writers, began the study of her own language after she was twenty, and another Turkish
lady, who spent a year in London when her husband
was attached to the Ottoman Embassy, is working
day and night at Turkish in order to write.

The hall in which the feminist meeting was
held was the large lecture hall of the university,
lent by the men. Men were the stewards, and all
four speakers were men. Strange and chivalrous
as it seemed to me to see the men conducting the
women's meeting, I was, however, disappointed
not to hear a woman speak. I had so often heard
of Halidé-Hanoum's talent as a speaker, and I
particularly wanted to compare her gestures, her
delivery, and her subject-matter with the women
speakers of my own country. Halidé-Hanoum is
the mother of two children. Up till a month ago
she taught history, pedagogy, and literature at the
Normal School for Girls. She has written five or

six volumes of importance, as well as articles on special subjects, and frequently she addresses the Friday afternoon meetings. But in all her work, she tells me, she has been encouraged by the opposite sex, and no one ever questions whether, since she gives so much time to public work, her children and home are neglected, as is generally the case with us.

Long before the meeting began the big hall was crowded with veiled women, a few of whom never raised their face veils during the whole three hours' meeting. The hall, from the entrance, appeared as if it were filled with nuns, for even those who had their veils thrown back carefully covered their hair. I was seated in the middle of the hall, with the Turkish woman who recently studied at Bedford College on my left, to translate for me, and my friend on my right, also to translate if she felt inclined.

The first person whom the chairman called upon to address us was a poet. Being unable to understand more than the titles and the ideas of the poems, I listened to the rhythmic language and watched the interested faces of the listeners. This poet, my friend explained to me, was a prominent member of the society, or rather, shall we call it the movement of " Turkey for the Turks "? One of the objects of this movement is to purify the language, to use exclusively Turkish words instead of a mixture of Turkish, Arabic, and Persian, which takes away from the strength of the

language and makes the study of Turkish so
difficult even for the Turks. We Westerners
forget that, besides French and English, and
perhaps German, cultured Turks must learn three
Oriental languages.

Another object of this Nationalist movement
is to encourage the translation of the Koran into
Turkish. The Koran has never been completely
translated into Turkish ; commentaries only have
been made, many of which have lost the spirit of
the Prophet's meaning. When once the Koran
is translated, when once the people can read,
think, and interpret for themselves the meaning
of the Prophet, then really will serious progress
begin.

I have been studying with a friend the verses
in the Koran concerning women. " Women
must have similar rights to men," says the Koran.
" Women are the twin halves of men—the rights
of women are sacred. The best of men are those
who are best to their wives. To acquire knowledge is an equal duty of man and woman.
Woman is the sovereign in the house of her
husband." " Whosoever doeth the things that
are right, whether male or female, they shall enter
Paradise." This is all so strange to me, I who
have heard, ever since I can remember, that
Mahomet denied woman even a soul, and she
could not go to Heaven unless her husband cared
to take her there.

We read, too, the verses on veiling. " Mahomet," my friend explained to me, "knowing the jealous temperament of the Arab, considered it wiser for *married* women to veil their hair, but he did not say all women were to be veiled, that is an amendment tacked on by his followers, and it is they, and not the Prophet, who are responsible for this useless bondage."

I have discussed with many enlightened Turkish women this question of the veil. Is it a protection or is it not? Halidé-Hanoum considers it creates between the sexes a barrier which is impossible when both sexes should be working for the common cause of humanity. It makes the woman at once "the forbidden fruit," and surrounds her with an atmosphere of mystery which, although fascinating, is neither desirable nor healthy. The thicker the veil the harder the male stares. The more the woman covers her face the more he longs to see the features which, were he to see but once, would interest him no more.

Personally I find the veil no protection. In my hat I thread my way in and out of the cosmopolitan throng at Pera. No one speaks to me, no one notices me, and yet my mirror shows I am no more ugly than the majority of my sex. But when I have walked in the park, a veiled woman, what a different experience. Even the cold Englishman has summed up courage and enough Turkish to pay compliments to our "silhouettes." We have not heeded them, walking as real Turkish

women, with stooped backs and bent heads and a
rather swinging gait, but these two silent figures
only served to excite their curiosity, and no doubt
they wondered at my thick veil. . . .

Another reason for condemning the veil is that
it dispenses women from taking the responsibility
of their actions.   Should they desire to stray
away from the path of virtue, who can control the
actions of these black-robed, veiled women ?
During the reign of Abdul Hamid they helped
most considerably in bringing about the Revolution, for it was they who went from house to
house carrying the letters, as the men never could
have dared to do.   It was the women who were
responsible for nominations being cancelled and
for many important appointments, and even I
have seen before now veiled women pleading the
cause of their mankind at the feet of a Grand
Vizier's daughter.   Turkish men and women now,
however, have both declared that an anonymous
power is a danger to the State, and yet who is to
be the first woman to leave off her veil ?

But to return to the speakers at the meeting.
The poems, in beautiful sounding language, were
an appeal to the women to save the Fatherland,
and again and again I recognized that sacred
word.   The poet, with a woeful face, outstretched
arms, and tearful voice, pleaded till most
of us had melted into tears.   This recent war
had touched all those women so closely, most
of them had lost some loved ones during the

war, many of them had nursed those who were wounded and had fallen victims to cholera, but always the word Fatherland brought home to them the terrible fact that half the Fatherland was no longer theirs.

The next speaker was more philosophical and scientific. We dried our eyes and listened. He was explaining to us the value of our sex from a scientific point of view, and he tried to show the impossibility of one sex raising itself without the assistance of the other. "Am I really in Turkey?" I frequently asked myself, as the principal points of the speaker's utterances were translated to me. It is as if sometimes when I think of my home away yonder and my fellow-women workers that I am standing on my head. "We are at the Antipodes, we English and Turks," a Pasha once said to me. Indeed, he was right. Was there ever, I wonder, in my country a feminist meeting conducted only by men and where the men urged the women to rebel and strike for freedom? . . .

The third speaker had been in England, and prefaced his plea of "Turkey for the Turks" by relating some of his experiences in our capital. "On one occasion," said he, " I had been invited to listen to music performed by petticoated soldiers. But it was more horrible than anything I ever heard. Our Kurds would have been ashamed of such a performance!" On another occasion he visited a school; the teacher asked the assembled boys to guess the speaker's nationality. Unable to guess, they had to be told he was a Turk. "And then," said the speaker, "the little boys uttered a cry of alarm." "Why are you frightened?" asked the teacher. "Turks eat little boys," was their reply. The speaker was not at all enthusiastic about my country; he felt so hurt at being asked the usual questions about the harem life, and how many wives he had, that he finally refused, he said, to converse with such ignorant people. He spoke, too, of the grinding poverty of the East End of our capital. "How dare that nation criticize us," he added, "when within the gates of their own city people are living in a manner unworthy of a civilized nation." He was right, this speaker, much as I wish he could have left unsaid what he had, alas! seen.

From afar we appear to the foreigner so great and magnificent, but when once they have stayed in our capital, and seen for themselves the degradation of our people, there is always a blot on the picture, and England is never for them the England they had dreamt of and wished to see. The object of this speech was naturally to prove the futility of any longer admiring a people who took no pains to hide how little they respected the Turks. "We must learn to help ourselves. God helps those who help themselves," was his concluding remark. These Young Turks have certainly begun to learn the wisdom of action.

The last speech, however, was the speech which stirred the women most. How I wish it had been possible to read it afterwards in French, for my neighbours, after two and a half hours' constant translating for me, began to grow just a little weary, and I could see they wished to listen to every word. The speaker had no notes, but he spoke with eloquence and a passion I have never yet seen in a man pleading a cause not his own. His subject was " The veil and the subjection of women." He condemned it from a moral point of view, and he condemned it from a physical point of view, and showed how, in spite of the custom which has been accepted now for centuries, veiling is against the teaching of the Koran. " Our Prophet," said he, "considered ignorance a sin. What has been done to help you out of ignorance ? "

A woman, according to the Koran, may preach in a mosque, and may exercise any profession she chooses. How have you taken advantage of these privileges ? Then he blamed the woman. " Can you not feel your bondage ? " he asked. " Who can give you freedom unless you yourselves ask for freedom ? What right have the interpreters to bind and fetter and degrade women ? I am not against religion; it would be disastrous for Turkey to-day if there were no religion; but what I demand, and what every thinking man and woman should demand to-day, is a reformed religion, a seeking after the truth, the

real meaning of the Prophet's teaching." A
storm of applause greeted these words. My
friend translated. I watched the women with
their veils down over their face. Surely, after
such a speech they would throw them back.

I, the foreigner, was stirred ; it seemed to me
that after such a speech I would be capable of
any action to be free . . . there sat the women,
a handkerchief occasionally poked behind the
thick veil, to wipe away their tears, but never
once were their veils lifted. How well he had
spoken ! How necessary, indeed, in this country
is a reformed religion ! How extraordinary it
is that everywhere the Church is the chief oppo-
nent to most reforms ! Has the Christian Church
given to woman the place that Christ intended
her to have? How has the Church helped the
women of my country in their fight for freedom ?
A little mild assistance when the heavy spade
work is done, perhaps, is better than no assistance
at all. . . .

Unfortunately for the women here, the theatre
at present is too primitive to be of any practical
assistance. I do not mean, of course, the poor
French companies which visit Pera almost weekly,
but the little native theatres to be found right
in the heart of Stamboul, and which my friends
have visited since I have been staying with them.
Whatever piece is played at these little theatres
becomes ridiculous by the mere fact that when an
Armenian cannot be found to play the part of

a Turkish woman, a man has to supply that need, and that in itself turns any play into a farce. It is not easy either to find an Armenian to play the part of a young Turkish girl. Her accent is not pleasant, so I am told; her voice exceedingly disagreeable; and I personally saw a woman whom no theatrical manager would have accepted in my country, except for the rôle of a stout, elderly matron, playing the part of a coy maiden of fifteen.

This, of course, made the piece worthless except as an amusement, and a form of amusement a trifle too primitive for thinking women to-day. "How can I convince these people?" one day a Turk asked me. "Have you ever tried the theatre?" I asked in reply. "In our Western countries it is from the stage that most of our important messages are given to the world—the stage has been magnificent in the cause of women."

But to return once more to the meeting. "Can you not see for yourselves," went on the speaker, "that although it is our duty to protect our women, it is detrimental to their very best interests to keep them shielded from every gust of wind? What use are these hot-house flowers in the garden of life? Virtue cannot be purchased by slavery. Are you going to cut out your children's tongues to prevent their telling lies?" Again a storm of applause gave my neighbour a chance of translating for me. Then the meeting

ended.   How magnificently he had spoken!
After such a speech one would have expected
these women to have walked out without their
veils . . . but they are still afraid.

To ask a Turkish woman to go out without her
veil is almost like asking an Englishwoman to go
out without a blouse.   Living in a Turkish
household one sees this slavery has become
almost part of a woman's existence.   I have heard
of women face to face with death, women saved
from a burning house, covering their hair with
a veil—the height of imprudence.   The other day
at luncheon a poetess of about fifty was at the
table.   In the midst of a most interesting discussion on modern Turkish literature, she
screamed, and holding her serviette between
her face and the open door, called for a veil.
She had heard the young Bey's spurs coming
towards the open door of the dining-room.
" Don't come in!" called my hostess to her
husband, and at last I understood what was
happening.

I was wearing a Broussa silk scarf round my
shoulders ; I lent it to her ; she covered up all her
hair and tied it round her neck ; then the young
Bey came in to lunch.   And yet this was not an
ignorant woman !   On the contrary, she was a
woman of great intelligence, but she, like so
many others, will not countenance any attempt
to modify the veil.

And what about the other women ?   Halidé-

Hanoum, who tells me "the veil surrounds the woman with an unhealthy air of mystery"—how does she appear in the street? A thick veil over her face, which she never throws back. I asked her one day the reason why she kept herself so closely veiled. "It is a habit," she answered. Another feminist told me of her great admiration for the British militant Suffragettes. "If only we Turkish women could get some of that fine spirit," she said; and a little while later she told me of an adventure she had had a few days before. It was towards five o'clock, an insolent Turk had pulled her sleeve and pinched her arm. She was defending herself with her umbrella, when the policeman came to her assistance. "And what happened?" I asked, for she stopped short in her narrative. "I am ashamed to say," she answered, "I ran away. If I had stopped to give evidence the man would have been exiled." "And what an advertisement for your cause," I added. "Yes," said she, "but I had not the courage to face the scandal!"

As I have said before, it is not for me to criticize the methods of the women of a civilization so totally different from our own. The men are urging them to take their freedom, and helping them all they can, but if they will be free they themselves must strike the blow. The women of another civilization cannot help them except by giving them the benefit of education whenever they ask for it. An enterprising Turkish woman came a

year ago to Bedford College to study.   Her year
in England will mean more to her than anything
that could have been offered to her.   She may
not have learnt from us as much book knowledge
as the French could have taught her, but she took
away with her a moral background which is of
more value than mere knowledge.   I have seen
this woman giving her lessons.   I have seen her
when her weekday lessons are ended spending
her Friday (the Turkish day of rest) giving
lessons to the women of the poor classes.   Some
of these women are between fifty and sixty, some
are younger, but it is one of the most pathetic
sights I have yet seen here to see these old ladies
spelling out their words like little children, and
with bent backs applying themselves to the task
of learning to write as if their very existence
depended on it.

When once women can be seriously interested
in a cause they are splendid.   In Turkey, in
spite of their veil, in spite of their apparent
desire not to take advantage of the privileges
offered them, they have shown themselves magnificent in two most important branches—nursing
and teaching.   In both these branches the Turkish
woman has shown qualities Europe never supposed she possessed—she is a true patriot.

CHAPTER VII

PASSIONATE WOMEN PATRIOTS—A
MASS MEETING

THIS is the anniversary of the foundation of the Ottoman Empire—a red-letter day for Turkish feminists. To-day for the first time the various women's societies have held a mass meeting, and a member from each society has given an account of the year's work. This meeting, then, marks the end of the old régime for the Turkish woman. She has now given us, as it were, chapter and verse as to the rôle she intends to play in the future. She has cast aside the dangerous rôle she played until quite recently —a powerful part, and all the more powerful since it was anonymous. When anything went wrong with the political pie into which so many of them had put their fingers—it was not a case of "cherchez la femme," for she disappeared behind the veil, and the men least of all suspected how well these women could ruin a cause if only they chose. Turkish women, then, are sacrificing a powerful anonymous rôle for an honest responsible part in the work of the world, and recognizing that only by straightforward, honest methods can they advance the welfare of humanity.   And so the Turkish women who declared themselves perfectly satisfied with their bondage, and yet at the same time worked in secret to break those chains, have now come out in the manner of the Western women, openly to demand their rights.

But it is unjust to give all the credit of this meeting to the women.   How different would have been their position now had they had a Government against them !   I am not going to put halos round the heads of the Young Turks, nor am I going to present them with a pair of angel's wings ;   such vain flattery would be as useless as it is bad form.   The Young Turk, however, has not yet had his opportunity.   Youth and inexperience are responsible for many strange blunders—effort is so new a chapter in the life-story of Turkey ;   effort and blunders beget experience, and experience he must have at all costs.   In his political methods he has not been impeccable.   I do not defend him.   What I do protest against, however, is that an action committed by a Turk should be called "a crime," and yet committed by a Christian neighbour "a diplomatic error."   And so in this question of women.   "See," says Europe, "how the Turk treats his women."   "See," I might answer, "how the British Government treats its women."

There are so many questions which should be entirely settled by women and never taken to the

Imperial Parliament at all. The Turkish Government has been wiser than we in this matter, for it recognizes that education and the housing of the poor are questions which should be left as much as possible in the women's hands.

A Turkish Feminist Government! To Western Europe this sounds strange. We have heard for so long of the Paradise of Mahomet, where women have no place, and of a religion which does not credit them even with the possession of a soul. Exactly how these ideas originated no one has been able to tell me—perhaps in the imagination of Hood, for the Koran distinctly states that " Paradise is at the mother's feet." A Turkish Feminist Government! Have the women quite become accustomed to the idea? It is true they never before possessed such privileges. One of the first triumphs of the counter-revolution of April 13 was the total destruction of the woman's club founded by Selma Hanoum, sister of Ahmed Riza Bey, and that lady nearly lost her life as her reward for having espoused the cause of the liberty of her Turkish sisters.

This meeting, which celebrated the foundation of the Ottoman Empire, was under the patronage of Djémal Pasha, now General Pasha and Minister of Public Works, to whom I have so often referred as the Military Governor of Constantinople. When congratulating him on his new appointment, I asked him if, in his new capacity, he would still be the " feminist " Minister. " Most

6

certainly," said he ; " this whole Eastern question, is it not a woman's question ? "

He it was who gave women the opportunity of visiting the warship *Hamidieh* ; he who allowed a Turkish woman, Belkis Chefket Hanoum, to go up in an aeroplane, and then had her portrait placed in the Military Museum beside the heroes of Turkey ; he it was who had the State Treasury and old Serail opened for the first time for Turkish women. They have now sold at a charity bazaar ; they are organizing a concert, at which they will be allowed to perform. It seems hardly comprehensible to Western readers that these favours should be a question to be decided by a Government, or that such elementary every-day occurrences should be counted as steps towards freedom ; they should have been in Constantinople under the régime of Hamid, then they could take these " reforms " at their proper value.

Every place in the theatre where the meeting was held was crowded long before the time announced for its starting. There were no men in the audience, but men took part in the proceedings and made brilliant feminist speeches. The whole aspect of the audience was so different from anything I had seen in the West—the black-robed and veiled women, some puffing away contentedly at their cigarettes, others walking up and down to soothe their restless babies. Babies at a meeting such as this astonished me. I made the remark to my friend. They were not the

women of the "mothers' meeting" class, as many
would have supposed judging according to our
Western habits, but simply mothers who were
interested in the welfare of the country, and
curious to hear what was being done for the uplifting of their sex, but who at the same time
could not make up their minds to leave "the
baby at home." It was a curious conflict between
the woman of the old and new civilizations, which,
although so natural to my Turkish colleagues,
interested me more even than the accounts given
by the various societies of the work done.

It is unfortunate not to be able to understand
the language of the country one is visiting—this
was the first time I had ever heard Turkish
women speak in public, and I had to rely on the
assistance of an interpreter. They all seemed to
speak, however, without difficulty, quite simply,
with few gestures, no notes, and perfect calmness
until they came to the sacred word, "fatherland"
—then there were tears in their voice as well as
in their eyes.

How magnificent is this patriotism of the
women! There is a strong movement of patriotism amongst the men, but nothing to be compared with that wonderful "Joan of Arc"-ism
which is going on amongst the women. With
the men it is a mourning for their lost honour,
a desire for revenge. On coming out of the
military college at Broussa I saw each boy pause
before an image, which I from the distance mis-

took for the " Sacred Heart." How had this
" Sacred Heart" come into a Moslem college,
I wondered ; but on closer inspection I found it
to be the heart of the fatherland, pierced and
bleeding, and above it the map of the Ottoman
Empire, with its lost provinces covered in black
crêpe. Each boy, I repeat, paused, his brow
clouded, his chin was set firm, and then he placed
in the collecting-box his " mite " for the national
defence.

With the women the patriotism has the same
foundation of giving to a cause (far, far more
than they can afford they have given to the fund),
but a woman's patriotism is more complete than
that of a man—there is in it a mixture of fine
religious feeling, a pious cult for traditions and
responsibility as mothers of the race. Woman is
the destiny of man, and the Turkish woman,
because of her lack of education and her cloistered
condition, has been unable to give to the country
the men it needed. All this was explained in the
speeches. All her shortcomings the Turkish
woman recognizes—this is the beginning of her
salvation.

Another feature of this meeting which interested and surprised me was to see how cleverly
the Turkish woman is able to raise money and
how willingly her sisters respond to her appeal.

The seats for the meeting were from five francs
downwards, the entrance money being devoted to
the upkeep of a school for girls that women have

recently opened. They are responsible for the expenses of the school. During the afternoon "Alexandra roses" were sold in the same manner in which they are sold in my country for the benefit of the poor refugees, by whom they are made, and finally, after the principal speeches, a collection was taken in the real "Pankhurst" style for the national defence. I might almost have been back in London hearing the "militant" speakers pleading for funds for the "war chest."

"The nation must have a fleet, its very existence depends on its fleet, and the women must help," began the speaker. "I trust the women to give whatever they can." There was a moment's silence, a thrill went through the audience. What was coming? One of the charms of Turkish life is that you never know what will happen. Anything may happen, and generally that which is least expected. There was another pause. All eyes were fixed on the stage, for coming through the wings appeared a Turkish woman, wearing the white sash of the Navy League, and carrying in her arms what I supposed to be a baby in long clothes. Slowly and reverently she began to take off its silk wrappers, reverently she handed it to the chairman—it was not a baby at all, but a magnificent head of woman's hair, sent with these words, "This is all I can give towards the Turkish fleet."

As a rule Turkish women have very beautiful hair. Mahomet regarded a woman's hair as her "crowning glory," and it was for this reason he considered it wiser for married women's hair to be veiled; it is not a woman's face, but her hair the fanatics insist on having covered, and, as I have already explained, it is almost indecent to appear before a man with one's hair unveiled. One day I had strayed through the selamlik, and had gone bareheaded to the door. An employee had arrived at the door at the same time, and seeing me turned his head discreetly away until I had time to pull my *écharpe* over my hair. Hair, then, having this value attached to it, this extraordinary contribution towards the Turkish navy had a special meaning for the Turkish women. And the giver? Was she married? If so, her gift was of even greater value, since physical charm is the Turkish woman's dowry. Was she the wife, sister, or daughter of a Turkish officer? She preferred to remain anonymous with true Turkish modesty, and £80 was raised for the fund from the sale of her hair.

Dear little patriot! Every time I see in the papers the Turks have bought a new ship I shall think of her. Those ships to me have now taken a form different from mere ships, for have I not seen them purchased with the price of a woman's hair, the widow's mite, and the orphan's halfpence? But not only a woman's hair—

jewels, embroideries, stuffs were sold for the ships that were to " guarantee the very existence of the fatherland." Most women were weeping. Who could help it when mothers with bowed heads and broken hearts came forward with offerings such as this: " £5 I give to the National Defence in memory of my five sons fallen for the fatherland " ?

And so the moments I am spending in Turkey in the charming intimacy of my Turkish sisters are at bottom moments of sadness. Only five years ago I saw this people strike for freedom and shout with joy at the proclamation of the Constitution ; now after only five years they are in the deepest mourning. It is not in a fashionable hotel at Pera that one can understand the real meaning of the war. Never shall I forget the spectacle of a long procession of soldiers crossing the Galata Bridge. Medical science had done its best for these men, snatched almost, as it were, from the jaws of death. Of what use were they in life ? One person more to feed, and an eyesore to their nearest and dearest, one really begins to wonder if the old Chinese method of hacking the enemy to pieces is not, after all, the most merciful. There were men without legs ; some without hands and arms ; some blind ; but these were nothing compared to the hideously disfigured faces of many, and some of those earless or eyeless victims of the " Christian " Bulgars. No words can describe their pitiful condition—these men

had been mutilated for their fatherland, a glorious
destiny indeed. Should we not rejoice? At the
sight of them I was physically ill.

But there is another side to the question.
These men, many of them, were the bread-
winners. Who is going to feed the women now?
Now is the time to blame the harem system.
The idle, protected women, what are they going
to do now? In other countries women of this
class could cook or sew or clean. I would have
been glad of some one to sew for me besides
Miss Chocolate, but in all Stamboul, amongst all
these starving women, I can find no woman to
do plain sewing. It is not when women are
actually starving that one can teach them a trade;
they must work at once. They can embroider;
they can produce embroidery that is worth leaving to one's grandchildren, and yet a European
child of ten would be ashamed to make button-
holes as they do.

And this priceless embroidery is less well paid
than plain needlework in my country. The Red
Crescent Society undertakes to pay one franc a
day to these poor women who embroider and
weave, and also to find work for the poor refugees
who have come back penniless to their native
land rather than lose their nationality. It is sad
to see these poor creatures arriving. I have
been with the women of the Red Crescent Society
to meet them at the boats or outside the mosques,
where they sit and wait, whilst their husbands

try to get work. They look perfectly resigned, these poor women, as they sit huddled up beside the carpets and the cats, kept in bird-cages. Those who have no baby to nurse sit with their elbows on their knees and their heads on their hands. They can only wait their fate. But the Red Crescent ladies are there; they will not starve.

I had no idea before coming here of the splendid self-sacrifice these women are making for these starving souls. They have formed a league and have undertaken to buy only the stuffs of their own country, and have opened a shop in Stamboul where only Turkish goods are sold. No more Paris dresses, no more jewels; not one luxury till these poor, starving women are fed, and if you ask a Turkish woman to-day what is her greatest ambition, she will answer without hesitation, " To save my poor country."

I have no space in this book to write of the other works started by women, but the Red Crescent, which is organized on the lines of the Red Cross Society (and has the embroidery and weaving establishment in addition), and the movement for the education of the women are, to my mind, the most important of all. It is when one sees these women themselves fettered by atavism, crippled for want of education and a misunderstood teaching of the Koran, fighting against the terrible odds of having to find work for

women who cannot work, and food for hungry
mouths in a country where there is no money,
that one understands how bitterly these women
resent the manner in which they are introduced
by the writer's imagination to the Western
world.

I very much doubt whether, in the West, we
could have fought this terrible fight against
poverty as the Turkish women have done. It
is infinitely comforting, however, to think, as I
sink at nights into my comfortable cushions,
that although the wind is howling and the rain
is beating against the windows of this konak,
any beggar may come in and find food and shelter
in the basement. "Find me one of your Western
countries," said one day to me Zeyneb (Pierre
Loti's disenchanted heroine, to whom everything
Western now is tarnished by a lack of Christian
charity), "where the poor are accommodated in
the houses of the rich; and if they were," she
added, "you would have to employ a detective
to watch them."

CHAPTER VIII

A TURKISH MOTHER

I HAVE been this afternoon with Fâtima buying
" birth " presents. In a Moslem house it is
difficult to find a more appropriate name for these
presents, which correspond to our christening
presents. These " birth " presents, however, were
not only for a little new arrival in this world, but
for the dear friend to whom this little life was to
be entrusted.

This custom of honouring the mother as well
as the child, insignificant though it may seem, is
only one of the few ways in which homage is
paid to the mother in the East. Here all
maternity is respected. Not only the married
mother, but the unmarried mother, is respected,
so that the woman who is left with the " child
of her shame " to do the best she can for it and
herself does not exist yet in Turkey. It is
true the Turks do not consider their women
" responsible " for either their good or bad conduct, however much freedom Islam gives them.
In this, as in most things, we and the Turks
are at the Antipodes. According to the Moslem

law, a woman has absolute control of her own fortune ; she can exercise any profession she likes ; but when it is a question of a misdeed— theft, for example—the husband is responsible. I do not defend the Turkish system—nor do I defend ours, and the Turkish women themselves now recognize they must be accounted responsible for their good and their bad deeds.

To understand the importance given to maternity, one must have lived for a while in the East. Mahomet placed maternity above everything else when he said " Paradise was at the mother's feet." In the highest circles and in the poor man's house the mother rules. As cadines (wives) the Sultan's legitimate wives do not count socially, yet if the son of one of them becomes Sultan, she then is the highest lady in the land—the Validé-Sultana, to whom all petitions from the women to the Imperial Master must be addressed. She is the head of the Ottoman Court, the only woman before whom the Sultan kneels.

And so in private life, the relations between mother and son are not the same as with us. There are always reverence and respect for her as well as love. She is not the " old mater," nor would he allow her to wait on him. However great a scoundrel a man may be, however deep his hands may be steeped in blood, he will rise when his mother comes into the room, kiss her hand, then raise it to his forehead as a sign of great respect, and inquire for the health of Annajim (my dear mother), and give her the seat of honour.

In the homes of the people, in the two-roomed cabins in Asia Minor, and where they still eat out of one dish, helping themselves with their fingers, the son will only take his share when he is sure his mother has taken a substantial helping. The law of Islam obliges a man to keep his mother, and his wife accepts this as a matter of course.

A young Turkish woman who marries and has her own establishment, as with us, is the exception rather than the rule, and, personally, amongst all the women with whom I am acquainted, I know no one who does not live either with her husband's or her own parents. Some parents make the stipulation before consenting to their daughter's marriage that she shall still live with them, and I have met some parents who have refused good marriages for their daughters simply because they could not allow them to leave their home. The Turkish mother urges her son to marry as soon as possible. He marries before he can even keep himself. His family sees nothing extraordinary in the fact that they have not only to keep him, but his wife and family.

"And the mother-in-law?" one naturally asks. The relationship between a Turkish mother-in-law and her daughter-in-law is quite different from the relationship existing in the West. My hostess and her mother-in-law remind me not a little of

Ruth and Naomi. The daughter-in-law treats her husband's mother just as she would treat her own mother, *i.e.* she has the same position towards her mother-in-law that she had towards her own mother before marriage. It is the mother-in-law who is the head of the house, the mother-in-law who sits in the place of honour, the mother-in-law who is first greeted, the mother-in-law who gives permission to do such and such a thing, and who is called by her daughter-in-law Hanoum Effendi (honoured lady).

My friend cannot understand how difficult it would be for a daughter-in-law in England to live with her husband's mother, nor can she understand the tactless Western woman who expects a mother-in-law, her superior in age and experience, to give over the household to her son's wife. " My turn will come, alas! only too soon," one lady said, " when I become a mother-in-law, then I expect my daughter-in-law to treat me as I have treated my husband's mother—to love and respect me, and not to make of me a subject of ridicule." I must say it is difficult to think of the sweet-faced woman who sits at the head of our table as a mother-in-law in the Western sense of the word. She effaces herself with exquisite tact; absents herself when she thinks her presence unnecessary—for example, at our harem tea parties; gives advice only when it is asked; and is always ready to show how grateful she is to have gained a daughter and not lost her son.

It is curious and astonishing to see this woman of another generation not understanding in the least her daughter-in-law's civilization and culture and yet accepting it as perfectly all right. After the midday meal her prayer carpet is taken out of the cupboard and laid for her on the floor of her room, her shoes are removed, she performs her ablutions, veils her hair, and prays in the picturesque manner of the East. She obeys the teaching of Mahomet in the letter and not in the spirit, yet if it enters her head to wonder why her daughter-in-law performs none of the prescribed religious duties she never makes a remark.

When the young Bey's brother officers dine with us she absents herself from the table, for although nothing would induce her to be present, she sees no reason for her daughter-in-law not presiding at the table. Is it, I wonder, a broad mind which understands without understanding, or is it a supreme trust in her son, that he will only allow his wife to do those things which are right, or is it fatalism, a resignation to put up with what you cannot change? At any rate, the smooth working of a ménage of women of totally different centuries, the possibility of their living together in perfect peace and affection, shows there must be sacrifice on both sides, and a tact and diplomacy, which we do not possess.

It might be argued, the Turkish bride is of the mother-in-law's choosing. Generally yes, but not always. In a marriage *à la Turque* the bride-

groom takes on trust her whom his mother chooses
for him.   He is usually content with the choice,
or, if he is not, he accepts her as his written fate
and makes the best of the situation.   But since
the Turkish man has become accustomed to
Western civilization he no longer will marry
à la Turque, and since the customs of the country
do not allow a man to see and speak with the
woman he is to marry, many of them prefer to
marry a European.

A Turk recently told me you could not expect
thinking Turkish men to make a real Turkish
marriage.   He does not want a plaything—he
wants a companion, and Europe affords him the
possibility of at least knowing the woman he is to
marry.   To me it seems a dangerous and unsatis-
factory way of solving the woman question.
Turks who have acted otherwise have in general
linked their existences with that of not the best
class of European society, to put it rather mildly.
In fact, so serious did it become that a short
while ago the then Turkish Minister of Foreign
Affairs issued an order forbidding Turkish diplomatists to marry without the consent of their
Government.   Truly a wise measure.   All details
are required by the Turkish Government of the
young lady's Embassy, and marriage without
the Government's consent means dismissal from
the service.

When the Turkish woman has a foreign
daughter-in-law, the ménage does not always run

on smooth lines. The European is unable to adapt herself to her new surroundings, she does not take the trouble to understand the working of an entirely new civilization. . . . I have in these cases, however, always admired the forbearance and tact of the Turkish woman.

The modern Turkish woman demands the privilege of talking with her future husband before her fate is signed and sealed. She does not have the opportunity of knowing him as we Englishwomen know our future husbands, but she can at least know whether he will " get on her nerves," in which case she refuses to marry him. Judging, however, as she still does, by instinct, she generally chooses at least a man whom she can respect and a man whose physical appearance pleases her. Many women, however, have owned to me that they accepted their husbands not with any feeling of gratitude or delight, but rather with one of profound thankfulness they were no worse.

Most emphatically I disapprove of marriages between men of the East and women of the West, not because I do not think Turkish men good husbands and fathers, not because I do not consider them honest, upright men, but because I always see in one of these unions, if not disaster for the young couple themselves, at least disenchantment for the children of these unions.

When discussing this subject seriously with a

7

Turkish man who honoured me by asking my advice about his proposed marriage with a foreign lady, he confessed he preferred to marry a Mohammedan lady, but the " veil " placed too many obstacles in the way of his enjoying her companionship. " Why not marry a Turkish woman and give her her freedom ? " " No," he answered, " the women must go slowly; I shall be in my grave before they are free."

If ever Turkish women wanted an argument in favour of a strong militant movement, they have it in the colossal egoism of men like these. Had she the courage to break her fetters, then he would honour her with his protection, but since she has not, the foreigner, often the Turkish woman's social inferior, becomes his life companion. The law of Islam, at least a bad interpretation of the law of Islam, refuses to allow a Turkish woman to marry any but a Mohammedan, whereas a Moslem man may marry a Christian woman ; the woman now understands the slight this is to her sex and intelligence.

Since Turkish women cannot retaliate, then, by marrying a man of the West, how are they to accept the challenge other than by fighting for freedom ?

I have so often sighed here for the daring of some of my countrywomen, inconsistent as it may seem. What these women need is a strong woman at their head—a strong, responsible woman, with a definite programme, and able to gain the confidence of her sex. It is the circumstances which make the hero or heroine. "I am such an one as my age requireth," says the Book of Judith. It was the Hamidian régime which made Enver Pasha—there will come, most surely, a woman leader, and that moment may not be far off.

With a feeling of thankfulness that her husband is no worse, the Turkish woman (there are exceptions, of course) naturally stakes everything on maternity. That there should be women in the West who actually refuse to have children is incomprehensible to my friends, and that there are women who for the sake of their figures give their children to strangers to nurse is almost as incomprehensible.

"What have we Eastern women in common with you women of the West — not even the heart," said one day a Turkish woman to me as she caressed the little curly-headed girl who played at her knees. She added, "All my life's happiness is in that little form; my greatest sorrow was when I found it was physically impossible to nurse her, and every time I hear her call her foster-mother 'Anna' (mother), a name no doubt she deserves, I have just a tiny pain at my heart." And yet how good she is to this poor peasant woman. She had been deserted by her husband, her own child died a few days after its birth. "You understand," she went on, " she will stay with me as long as ever she likes.

She has been too good to my child for me ever to leave her without a home."

Aïche-Hanoum, the mother-to-be, for whom we bought presents, has been the subject of conversation for weeks past. To her all kinds of delicacies are sent, the most comfortable place is reserved for her in the harem, there is always some one to tuck her up amongst the cushions. How tenderly she is spoken of, how tenderly she is spoken to . . . in a short while Aïche will be called to fulfil the divine mission (according to the East) for which every woman was sent into the world. Then her outlook on life will be different. She will have a different position towards her friends ; it is almost as if she had, as it were, risen in the social scale.

.   .   .   .   .

We went to visit Aïche, the very day the little new arrival was expected. " In all probability we shall stay all night," said my friend before we started. " But shall we not be in the way ? " I asked. " Of course not," she replied. " How happy Aïche will be to feel we are there ; we Turkish women always take part in one another's joys and sorrows."

With my British fear of being in the way where I was certainly of no use, I took my place with the other six friends of Aïche who had come to be present at this very important moment in her life's history.

We were seated round the big mangol alternately drinking coffee (which we ourselves made on the red-hot charcoal), smoking and eating sweets. Two of the ladies had bound their heads up with handkerchiefs to prevent their having headaches, a precaution I did not imitate however much my friends advised me to do so. We did not speak. We just sat round the mangol waiting, waiting. . . .

I occupied the most comfortable of the *mussaffir's* rooms (guests' rooms) that night, for the other guests' beds were made on mattresses on the floor, in the Eastern unceremonious fashion. I should have preferred to occupy one of these " emergency " beds—they are perfectly comfortable—for in the guests' room when I finally sank to rest after the safe arrival of the little girl, I had the same uncomfortable feeling of the unnecessary trouble I was giving.

But the Eastern woman has not yet begun what we in the West know as "the servant trouble." With the abolition of slavery, however, this is on its way. When all the slaves in Fâtima's family are married, she must necessarily employ hired domestics ; with education " hired domestics " become *exigeants.* They will object to making coffee and emergency beds at all times and at all hours, then " good-bye " to the charming unceremonious hospitality of the East. . . . I asked a Turkish lady who had lived for some months in London what she most appreciated in our capital. "What I know best," she answered, "is Mrs. ——'s registry office for servants."

The next afternoon a host of friends and acquaintances arrived to pay a visit to the mother and the little girl. In my country the doctor and the nurse would have forbidden these visits as the height of imprudence; here "it is a matter of habit." It is true the visitors, in most cases, only passed in a procession before the mother and child, but even that seemed unnecessary fatigue for the mother, much as I was assured to the contrary.

The mother and daughter were picturesquely arranged. The mother, in her big bed, covered with a priceless embroidery, and the child, in a smaller bed, covered with a smaller quilt of the same priceless embroidery, peacefully sleeping, and a French Sister of Mercy, with her big white *cornet*, playing the part of nurse. It was a pretty picture—a picture which brought tears of emotion to the eyes of the visitors. It is an old and beautiful masterpiece—the mother and her child—all the world over, and a masterpiece at which every true woman looks again and again, and always with delight.

All the guests brought presents for the mother and child, according to their means. Some were of the greatest value—jewels, embroideries, stuffs—and Fâtima tells me her "birth" presents formed a very important part of her trousseau. But why, at a Turkish birth ceremony, is cinnamon syrup given to the guests? No one can tell me. To me this beverage is the only unpleasant feature of a most charming ceremony.

They called her " Melek " (Angel), the little girl. I made a sign of the Cross on her little forehead. Her mother was pleased. And as I made that sign I wondered why our Western mothers are not honoured as they are in the East. Christ paid as high a tribute to maternity as Mahomet. Who is responsible for the misinterpretation of His words? Is it civilization, or is it the Church?

CHAPTER IX

WOMEN WRITERS OF TURKEY

THERE are not many, it is true, but there are Turkish writers and Turkish women writers. For so long, however, it has been the habit to condemn wholesale everything Turkish that most European nations have come to the inconsequent conclusion that there is no Turkish literature.

Say to the average European that you have started to study the Turkish language, and he will ask, " Unless you are to live in the country of what use is it ? They have no literature." How many times has that remark not been made to me ! Yet there are some very fine master-pieces, and it is to an English Professor, Professor Browne, of Cambridge, that we owe a five-volume study of the history of Ottoman poetry, an intensely interesting and fascinating book, which has followed me into the houses of my Turkish friends.

It seems extraordinary to make such sweeping assertions without giving chapter and verse. " Had the Turks had an Omar Khayyam, long ago Europe would have known it," says the Western critic; " Most certainly, had the Turk had the supreme good fortune to be translated by a Fitzgerald," one might reply.

But it is not for one without an accurate knowledge of Turkish to compare the relative values of the Turkish and Persian poets. The Turks for a long period of their literary history bowed before the Persian culture, and once having accepted their methods, without, perhaps, any really particular reason for doing so, they remained loyal and faithful to the Persian culture, as they remained loyal and faithful to Islam. I wonder, however, since I have been studying some of the masterpieces of this language with my Turkish friend, whether often the disciple did not become greater than the master—great enough, at least, to require no longer the master's example. And then, as Browne and Gibbs have written, " it was when the Ottoman Muse had flung off her golden apparel, which for centuries the Persians had embroidered with gold and precious stones, as a present for her, and put on the Turkish chalvar (pantaloons) and enturi (tunic), that she assumed an air of youth, which suited her perfectly, and all the poets of the time admired her."

When last I visited Turkey five years ago I felt the time was very near when the Turkish woman of culture would have to find some art by which to express herself. Beauty's characteristic

is a desire for self-manifestation.   The eternal
blue of the sky and sea, the glorious sunsets, the
silence, the solitude of an existence lived amongst
people of another century ; the strong draught of
idealistic pantheism there is in the religion of
Mahomet—all give birth to beautiful thoughts ;
the difficulty is to find a form of expression.

The Turkish woman is modest, as I have said
in other chapters, and her modesty leads her into
a lack of self-confidence which has been detrimental to her cause.   Unlike the women of
Western Europe, she has not inherited the tired
brain of tired ancestors ; she has now awakened
after centuries of rest, with a brain fresh and
ready for work, and it is astonishing to see the
ease with which she can learn.

And so it is in literature.   Many of my friends
can write verse, but they have not yet written
prose, and the five Turkish women who can now
lay claim to a place in the world of letters all
began by writing verse.

Of the work of these five writers it is really
unfair of me to speak, seeing I can judge their
work only by translation, and that not at all well
done.   My object rather is to draw attention to
the fact that they exist, and to induce those
Turkish women, as, for example, Zeyneb Hanoum,
who have a thorough knowledge of French, to
save their compatriots' literary honour in the
eyes of Europe by giving us good translations of
their work.

Halidé-Hanoum's " Handan," which has been
so widely circulated in her own land, is an
interesting study of the Turkish woman's mind
and life told in a series of letters. But how could
this writer let her work make its bow to the
Western world in its inaccurate, and often in-
delicate French translation? I have read no
other work of this writer, and I believe "Handan"
is not Halidé-Hanoum's best work. But the
writer herself! what an interesting person! A
slight, tiny little person, with masses of auburn
hair and large, expressive Oriental eyes, she has
opinions on most subjects, and discusses the
problems of the day in a manner which charms
one not so much on account of what she says, but
because it is so different from what one expected.
Strange it does seem that these women who have
been bound and fettered for centuries, when once
they begin to think, acknowledge in the world of
thought no boundaries and restrictions. Again
we and they are at the antipodes. We Englishwomen, who have a liberty of action the world
envies, think, as a rule, in conventional grooves.
With how many of my feminist countrywomen
could I have discussed the subjects I have discussed with my Turkish friends?

It would not be without interest, perhaps, to
notice how many Turkish women are to-day
reading Ellen Key. Ellen Key in a Turkish
harem naturally sounds a little alarming! But
this herald of feminism to come cannot do as

much harm as she might in an English home, for I very much doubt whether they—except, of course, women like Halidé-Hanoum—understand what she means.   It is true the titles " Love and Marriage," " The Century of a Child," are especially attractive to those women to whom the sentimental side of Western life appeals as being an unexplored territory, and I feel sure many have ordered the works of Ellen Key on the strength of their titles, and then cast them aside, to be read some other time.

" To the pure, all is pure," we say.   The Turkish women generally, to my mind, are more pure-minded, perhaps, than the women of any other nation.   This will certainly come as a surprise to many, who, with their erroneous ideas as to what a harem really is, still consider the women as beautiful, idle, intriguing creatures, and " passion " as the only drama that is played within its mysterious walls.   How is it, then, that Turkish women have acquired this purity ? I am not speaking of the ignorant women, who are innocent rather than pure, but the women who read and think.   The explanation, I believe, is to be found in the fact that from the age when they begin to think the Turks are taught that nature must be respected.

As soon as children begin to ask what we call " embarrassing questions," they are told the truth. Mothers do not speak in whispers about subjects which are " perfectly natural " ; from a very early age children know exactly what "maternity" means. All nature, then, being taken as a matter of course, the *arrière-pensée* does not even come into existence; hence purity. When first I arrived in Turkey, however, I must confess I was surprised to hear the conversations which took place before the children. Now I see its advantages. Natural curiosity, unsatisfied, becomes morbid curiosity; morbid curiosity becomes degeneracy.

I heard the following conversation between a mother and her six-year-old son: "Mother," asked the little boy, "would it be very wicked of me if I didn't want to marry?" "Yes," replied the mother, "it is the duty of all men to marry." "Why is it the duty of all men to marry?" next he asked. "So that mothers may have dear little boys like you," she replied.

Of the work of Fâtima Alié Hanoum I have read only one book, "Oudi" (The Lute Player), in a French translation, which has kept none of the Eastern grace and charm of this writer's work, for her compatriots, men and women, universally pay homage to her fine talent, her subtle perception, her clear and poetical style, and her endless historical knowledge. Fâtima Alié Hanoum is no longer a young woman. She has a kind face, which shows at once her good heart; she is small, pale, thin, and exceedingly active, and her eyes sparkle with enthusiasm as she discusses with you the subjects which interest her most. Fâtima Alié is a feminist. She is strongly in favour of women leading an active, useful life, and working at a profession if necessary, but she is decidedly opposed to the adoption of European fashions in literary style, as well as in clothing and furniture.

To her the picturesque stuffs of Broussa are worth more than all the wares in shops of Paris put together, and to her neat compromise between a dressing-gown and a dress which covers her un-corseted form and to her easy, if not elegant, slippers, she will remain faithful to the end of her days. But feminist though she is, she strongly opposes any attempt to modify the veil, not be-cause the veil has to her a religious meaning, but to her it is one of the traditions of her race, and therefore sacred. No woman in Turkey has made a more thorough study of the Koran than she, and I am grateful to her for the pleasant moments spent in her "real Turkish" house whilst she has explained to me the position of women in Islam. The daughter of Djevdat Pasha, the celebrated Turkish Patriot, Fâtima Alié Hanoum has inherited documents which will make her work particularly valuable to those who are interested in the history of the Ottoman Empire. She is shortly to publish a history of the last four reigns, and she is particularly qualified to do this, since she worked for so many years as her late father's secretary.

It is interesting, but nevertheless sad, to find in studying the history of the women of Islam that they, as we of the West, have lost so much of the power they once possessed. Let us imagine for an instant those olive-skinned, perfumed women of Arabia in their gaudy raiment (much in the fashion we are wearing to-day), half-gipsy, half-empress, even though they were in rags, listening to the preaching of Mahomet in the desert. Was it not to them particularly that he was preaching?

During the war they took their place beside their husbands, to whom they were faithful and devoted, and their deeds of daring would make our hair stand on end, we, the super-sensitive creatures of this century of half-tones and half-emotions! In time of peace these women were faithful and sweet creatures, kind to the stranger who sought the hospitality of their tent, the stranger who, unknown the night before, received from them enough to satisfy his hunger and to continue his journey. And the fact that they were women did not prevent their taking part in the great outer life around them. Mahomet's own daughter, known as the " Lady of Paradise," was one of the finest orators of the East.

During Charlemagne's reign, too, when Haroun-al-Rachid was Khalif of Baghdad, a woman, Zeyneb, was appointed professor of the University of Baghdad, and five hundred young men daily listened to her lectures on philosophy. Her reputation was so great that she was known throughout the East. Then there was Leyla,

the famous poetess, and Hind, the famous wit,
who was asked to define the worst of women
(her answer has stood the test of time and become
proverbial). " The worst of women is she," she
said, " who when begged to speak holds her
tongue, and when begged to hold her tongue
speaks."

There was about the fifteenth century, too,
a poetess, Mihri, to whom we owe the following
lines : " One day the loved one who was near me
questioned me about my love. I gave him my
soul, and he never spoke of it again." There
was the poetess Fituat, also, whose work is full
of sorrow and feeling, and who made for herself
so great a reputation as a woman of letters. To
understand her work, I am told, is like " taking
part in the death of the whole world and the
awakening of another." What an original criticism! And if you question the people of Asia
Minor even to-day they will tell you history
cannot find a greater attachment given to a woman
of letters.

And so on through the ages. I could quote
names of women who have done great work,
women who have taken their place beside men.
How is it they lost their power, and gradually
sank down to the state of the poor nonentities
whom Lady Mary Montagu visited? " Islam
alone is responsible," says the Western critic.
But this is false. Mahomet's mistake, perhaps,
as a legislator, was that he gave too many rights

to the mothers, and not enough to women who were not mothers. Perhaps, I repeat. At any rate, all that has most oppressed and crushed the Turkish woman comes, not from Islam, but from, I was going to say, Christianity; I prefer the word Byzantium. The latticed windows, the wrong meaning of the veil, the harem, the eunuchs, the fez, the very Crescent itself, are all survivals of that Byzantium which has stifled, for a while, the life and soul of this people of the desert.

There are three more women of whom I must speak as modern Turkish women writers: Leyla Hanoum, an old lady now, whose verses were several times recited to me. I cannot judge her as a writer, except to repeat that the Turks themselves admire her work, and that when told they have no literature they indignantly ask, " And Leyla Hanoum ? "

There is also the poetess Niguar Hanoum, Niguar, whose acquaintance I made at Monte Carlo after the proclamation of the Constitution. A woman of great charm and intelligence and an exceedingly hard worker, it is she herself who will translate her own beautiful lyrics into French and German.

Another woman whose talent has been very much appreciated in her own land is Eminé Semié, a sister of Fâtima Alié Hanoum. Her novels have not been translated. Her political articles have been of no little assistance to Young Turkey. I met this famous authoress first in

8

Paris ; it was during the recent war. Not one luxury would she allow herself, not even a cab in the pouring rain, and all her beautiful jewels she sold in order to send the money to the Red Crescent Society. She had worn herself almost to skin and bone as a Red Crescent nurse, and had been sent to Paris to recuperate. Her impressions of the gay capital were all so charming and original.

But I cannot close this chapter on the women writers of Turkey without speaking of " Kadinlar-Dunyassi " (" The Feminine World "), a weekly illustrated paper devoted to women's interests, whose pages are open to any woman writer who cares to contribute. It was started, first of all, as a daily illustrated paper—rather an ambitious idea, but as such it was a failure, and was therefore quickly converted into an illustrated weekly.

The proprietor and editress of the paper, Oulvyé Mevlane Hanoum, had had no experience whatsoever either of editing or of the business side of running a paper ; therefore, the result of her effort is doubly interesting. She understood that if a serious society for the advancement of women was to be founded they must have an organ in which to explain their views. She saw the need, and she supplied it.

The publication of this paper is a very happy omen for all those who take an interest in the woman question. It shows what Turkish women can do when they have confidence in themselves and a determination to succeed—unfortunately two qualities they rarely possess. I do not mean to say they are lazy, but they lack concentration certainly, and are too proud to risk a failure. But all this will change. Only by measuring ourselves against the great can we understand how they, too, have tried and failed over and over again, then we take courage.

What matters it whether the articles of "Kadin-lar-Dunyassi" are not equal to those published in the daily papers! If every Turkish word were badly spelt and every phrase badly constructed, and every article poor, I should still rejoice at the publication of "Kadinlar-Dunyassi," because it is a co-operative effort—co-operative effort alone can save Turkey.

And now where are those women who are seeking to express themselves to turn for assistance? To the West naturally, and to France. It was Shinasi Effendi who ended the Persian allegiance—Shinasi Effendi who took his countrymen to the West, and is rightly considered the founder of the modern school of Ottoman literature. The hazard which turned him towards the West is interesting, as showing on how slender a thread a great change may depend. Shinasi was born about 1826, in the Top-Hané division of Constantinople. After attending the parish school he entered the Imperial Arsenal, and when there made the acquaintance of the Comte de Châteauneuf, who afterwards became a Turk,

embraced Islam, and became known as Rechid
Bey. This Frenchman was the grandfather of
my friends Zeyneb[1] and Melek[2] Hanoums, the
heroines of Pierre Loti's " Désenchantées."

From Châteauneuf, who admired the intelligence of the youth, Shinasi received the French
lessons which created in him the strong desire
to become more and more intimately acquainted
with the culture of the West, and he never rested
till his great desire was accomplished and he
finally went to Paris. An interesting study might
be written of the career of this extraordinary
man, whose translation of the French classics,
especially of Voltaire and Rousseau, changed the
whole destiny of his country's literature and history. Just as the French expressed themselves
in French, so the Turks, after Shinasi, learnt
not to express themselves in Persian construction,
but to say what they wanted to say in a Turkish
construction.

After Shinasi came Ziva Pasha, the great
Kemal, who was exiled after the publication of
" Vatran " (" The Fatherland "), and who in his
writings paid so high a tribute to England : and
finally, the greatest of modern Turkish poets
and writers—Abdul-Hak-Hamid, for some time
at the Turkish Embassy in London. The
publication of his " Makber " (" Tomb ") com-

---

[1] Zeyneb.—Co-authoress of " The Turkish Woman's European
Impressions."

[2] Melek.—Co-authoress of " Adbul Hamid's Daughter."

pletely revolutionized Turkish literature. Shinasi
had shown the way : Abdul-Hak-Hamid took
it, and his verses are already Turkish classics,
recited in all the schools.

And now for the political side of Shinasi's
work. It is necessary for me to point out that
a careful study of Rousseau gave birth to the
Young Turk party, which overthrew the most
terrible absolutism the world has known, to my
mind more terrible even than the absolutism of
Nero.

The absence of what we in the West call
" social life " naturally makes the Turks great
readers, and the sale of French books in Turkey
is enormous. Books, good, bad, and indifferent,
are read, and there are some who blame the
" French novel" for all the shortcomings of the
Turkish youth of to-day.

Unfortunately, the number of persons who read
English is limited. I say unfortunately, because
the spirit of our literature is much better suited to
the Turkish character. It is astonishing to notice
how many qualities of the Englishman the " real "
Turk possesses, and particularly his *sangfroid* in
moments of difficulty and danger. In appearance,
too, many of them are so like my own countrymen (and particularly a naval officer whom I met
the other day), that one wonders often whether
they are not Englishmen in the Turkish service.

Although a translation is, after all, only the
wrong side of an embroidery, I have, wherever I

can, urged my friends, since they cannot read our masterpieces in English, to read them in the French translation.

The Turks may not quite agree with me, but it has seemed to me everywhere I went that our literature comes as a surprise to them. We have the reputation of being a solid, matter-of-fact, honest nation, with a mighty fleet. England still puts her hall-mark of "all-rightness" on everything she touches, but somehow literature and art are not expected of us. The Turks will tell you they have read our masterpieces, they know our literature . . . but I saw none in any of the libraries of the colleges I visited. Voltaire, Rousseau, V. Hugo, Vigny, Anatole France, Pierre Loti, and now a "promise" of Wells and Kipling.

I must add, however, in defence of the Turks, that this neglect of our literature is very largely our own fault. What have we done to spread the knowledge of our language in the near East? And what has France done? Les Dames de Sion, the Lazarists, and the innumerable other orders who, when driven from France, sought the hospitality of the kindly Turk, what have they not done to further the knowledge of their language, not only in Constantinople, but throughout the East? And we?

CHAPTER X

THE PROPHET AND POLYGAMY

NO book on Turkey would be complete without a chapter on polygamy—in justice to the Turk such a chapter is necessary. It is the chapter to which every reader will turn first of all, and not *one* critic will allude to it. How well I know my countrymen!

Let me at once confess, however, to the morbid curiosity of actually trying to find a "harem" where there was more than one wife. Fâtima wished to satisfy that curiosity if it were possible. "You must see us as we really are," said she and her husband, "and if this unfortunate blot on our civilization is still to be seen, you shall see it." And he really went out of his way, this kind, courteous host of mine, Fâtima's husband, to ask all and sundry where, in Constantinople, could be found two women sharing the protection of one lord and master, and for a long time not one was to be found.

I have met, however, men and women who are the children of fathers who had more than one

119

wife. They are too proud to speak of their unhappy youth, but since we find them in the front ranks of those who are standing for the elevation of womanhood, we must necessarily draw our own conclusions. One of the most beautiful of modern Turkish poems is written by a feminist orator, describing in touching, eloquent notes the tragedy of being a child in a polygamous household.

To me, the lover of the East and the admirer of Islam, this " permission " to have four wives is regrettably unfortunate. From that "permission " we have totally misinterpreted the words of the Great Prophet of the Desert ; we have classed Islam as a religion destined to encourage sensuality, a religion devoid of spirituality, a religion which has degraded womanhood, whereas, those who take the trouble to study particularly that part of the Koran relating to women must pay homage to the wonderful foresight of this great reformer.

When Mahomet limited the number of wives to four, he was legislating for a people which polygamy had reduced to the depths of degradation, and those who will compare the history of the period when Mahomet began his ministry and the period afterwards, must surely admit the high place given to women in his teachings and the excellent laws made for their protection.

The poor down-trodden woman of the East is one of the fallacies which has descended through the ages, and nothing has done more to increase the misunderstanding between East and West than the Western disdain for what, to the Oriental, is all that he counts most sacred—his women and his religion.

When Mahomet limited the number of wives to four, he was legislating for a people who could not be brought too suddenly from the outer darkness to the great blazing light of civilization, but he put what appear almost like codicils to annul the statement about polygamy when he ordained that each wife must be treated with an equal amount of tenderness, that man *and woman* must seek knowledge "from the cradle to the grave," and "that they must keep travelling about, for there were many beautiful things to be seen on God's earth." There is also that splendid verse which I hope my feminist friends will stretch to its utmost capacity : "You must march on with the centuries." Time and knowledge will put everything right, argued the Prophet. Alas! is it not the tragedy which accompanies the life-work of every great reformer for the meaning of his words to be misinterpreted ?

Mahomet in his time was confronted with a woman's problem as entangled as the woman's problem of to-day. Although he considered maternity the destiny of woman, he did not prevent her entering the professions. Few women, however, could work, and since she

could not work she had to be provided for.
Was it not better for four women to be
housed and cared for than for one to live in
luxury and three to starve? No man was
obliged to take advantage of the Prophet's permission to have four wives, but the Prophet,
with his keen knowledge of humanity, foresaw
the danger to which the woman might be
exposed, and polygamy was the loophole through
which her honour could be saved.

But now all this is changing. For some time
now polygamy has been very *mal vu*, and nothing
hurts a Turk more than the eternal Western
question : " How many wives have you? " An
officer on board the man-o'-war which brought the
Turkish Crown Prince to our Coronation tells me
that every Englishwoman with whom he danced
at the Naval Ball asked him that same question,
" How many wives have you? " And to every
one he replied : " Just one dozen, and I hope
to have one dozen more before I die." He was
a bachelor.

Polygamy is not amongst the Turks the same
smart smoking-room joke that it is in the West,
and I have heard these Turks who are working
day and night to save their country protesting
with energy against the " princely privilege " of
having more than one wife. " The whole system
will have to be changed, and the sooner the
better," a Young Turk said, and, even as I write,
the news comes to me that the Turkish Govern-

ment has passed a decree forbidding polygamy in the Imperial household and refusing to recognize as legitimate any but the children of the first living *wife*.

This is, perhaps, the most important reform that Young Turkey has so far brought about, a change which will do more than anything to heighten her prestige in Europe, and it is the first step towards the formation of a " court " as we in the West understand that word.

It was during the reign of Abdul Hamid that the absurd rule which allowed Royal princes only to marry slaves was so strictly observed. So terrified was the ex-Sultan, in particular, of giving power to a subject, through the alliance of his family with the daughters of Pashas or Imperial Princes, that the wives of the Emperors had to be chosen from amongst the slaves of the Imperial harem—from amongst those girls who had been bought at an early age on account of their physical qualifications *only*, and their Circassian parents being paid a sum down renounced any claim to these children. These girls were prepared for the rôle of Empress which they might one day be called upon to play, dancing and music being very important items in their education. Then they had to await such time as they might find favour in the " Master's " sight and become his favourites.

A ugly, unhealthy atmosphere surrounds this buying and selling of human beings after careful

examination of their teeth, hair, and skin, and the
Royal purchasers themselves are the first to complain about it.   How can an intelligent man be
expected to comply with such unnecessarily bar-
barous customs?   If it is imprudent to marry
the daughters of Pashas, have not Egypt and
India enough and to spare of Moslem Princesses
to grace the Ottoman throne?   So probably the
Imperial family has argued, for now for the first
time two Princes of the Imperial Ottoman family
are to marry the two daughters of the Governor
of Broussa, the nieces of the Grand Vizier, Prince
Said Halim, and nieces of the Khedive.

These two Princesses, although, like their
mother, "more Turkish even than the Turks,"
have travelled extensively, and are well read and
cultured women.   They have been brought up by
an English governess.   The Princess, their mother,
an artist to her finger-tips, refuses to modify in
any manner the sacred laws prescribed by the
Prophet, yet she accompanies her husband on
his official excursions into the interior of Asia
Minor, and takes a particular delight in the
study of the lives of those primitive peoples of
Turkey whose hospitality she accepts.   The
Princess pays visits to the mosques and tombs,
and what lover of art would not take the
opportunity of studying in detail the most exquisite colouring and designs of the porcelains
of those mosques, the Green Mosque in particular,
which Pierre Loti has immortalized?   Pierre Loti

used, the guardian of the mosque told me, to write his books in the Green Mosque, sunk in the magnificent carpets, the quality and beauty of which have defied time, with on one side of him the door (which replaces our altar) of exquisitely blended green porcelain and beautifully worked golden lettering, and on the other side the central fountain, which, from its multitude of invisible mouths, sends out a gorgeous mass of exquisitely coloured rainbows between you and the sun.

Before dawn Loti was in the mosque, working all day in the hallowed atmosphere of God's house, the kindly guardian bringing him coffee and his *narghili* when he required them, and arranging the cushions when he wished to sleep. Loti's best work was done in the Green Mosque at Broussa.   No wonder !

. . . . .

No one could dread more the advent of electric cars and light than the Princess.   " It will not be Broussa any more," she says, and rightly so, and yet the Princess herself is helping on progress— she has started schools in the town itself and in the neighbouring villages, she herself bearing the entire expense.   And the little girls are taught Western dancing, they sing Western songs, and recite Western poetry.   How is one to make a compromise between the two civilizations?   I sympathize, however, with the Princess in her reluctance to welcome such intruders as cars and electric light.   When once this tide of progress comes in it will sweep all before it. Historical associations will have to give place to hideous Western factories; smoking chimneys will obscure the sight of the minarets; but no longer shall we see the cabman tying up his back wheel with a cord to replace the brake. The students in the "Medressa" (college of Theology), the future Hodjas whom I saw busy washing their linen in the fountain, where will they be in the days of Western steam laundries?

.   .   .   .   .

It is very difficult to give accurate knowledge about members of the Imperial family, unless brought into intimate contact with them. Their subjects do not know them, and they multiply so quickly that it is easy for a stranger to credit princes with accomplishments they do not possess and overlook the qualities of those princes who deserve praise. Of some of the princes it would be charitable to guard a discreet silence, and, after all, so little is required of them: they cannot even play a "spectacular" part, as our Western royalties do. Therefore, says Young Turkey, and wisely so, the State can no longer afford to keep these ever-recurring princes: one family is quite sufficient for each member of the Imperial house, we will recognize no more.

To all those who stake any importance whatsoever on soul heredity, this Eugenic manner of arranging Imperial marriages is a dangerous experiment. Fortunately they were given Circassian wives, otherwise whence would so many Imperials have acquired their talents, charm, and moral qualities. And Abdul Hamid, the criminal genius and madman, the monster tyrant —how far was he responsible for his actions? Who can tell us the truth about his birth? Some say he was born of an Armenian dancer, others credit him with French blood, brought into the Imperial harem by a lady of that race, captured by brigands and sold into slavery. All kinds of suppositions are advanced to explain the curious mentality of this man, who still puzzles criminologists of the twentieth century.

Most sincerely is Young Turkey to be congratulated on this new and enormous step towards progress. It is a bold step. Any blow levelled against the dynasty, any modification of the "divine" rights of the Kalife, is liable to rouse ignorant fanaticism of those turban-headed masses in Asia Minor who still know neither the meaning of Kalife nor that of the Constitution, but would willingly die for both.

CHAPTER XI

THE MAN WITH TWO WIVES

I HAD given up hope of seeing a Turkish house where there was more than one wife. I was sorry, and Fâtima was sorry that she was unable to satisfy my curiosity. The opportunity came, however, when we least expected it.

We were sipping our coffee one day in the big salon. *Guzel Sutanna* (the beautiful nourrice), as I called Fâtima's nourrice to distinguish her from her little daughter's nourrice, had tucked us up comfortably amongst the cushions, and whilst distributing to us lumps of pumpkin preserve which she had made for our special benefit, she was recalling certain chapters of her own strange life-story which Fâtima translated for me.

I loved *Guzel Sutanna*. She was so superbly human. Sorrow had sweetened what was still a beautiful face, beautiful enough to allow one to guess what her beauty and charm had been. She had had six successive husbands. Her lords and masters, she confessed quite as a matter of course, had never been more to her than a means towards an end. Maternity was her rôle, not wifehood ; then God gave to her for a little while what the old nourrice called "the most precious of His angels," but death and the Imperial Harem took them all away from her, and in her old age she became what she had firmly made up her mind from girlhood she never would be—childless. Such is the irony of life !

And so Fâtima became the whole world to the old nourrice. She could have lived with us altogether, but her young master (for this old lady had married a man many years her junior), claimed a certain amount of her attention, yet she generally managed to come and see Fâtima every day, and always bringing with her some of her delicious violet and rose jams.

We had made up our minds that Fâtima's husband must try to obtain a diplomatic post and live for a while in England. I was teasing *Guzel Sutanna*, telling her in England her services would no longer be required, that I should look after Fâtima. But the old nourrice was not to be worsted. " Tell me," she said to Fâtima, " as soon as the appointment becomes official, then I will marry my husband to some one else and come with you."

The old nourrice had the form of a young woman. A green plaid dress covered her un-corseted body, around her waist she wore a gold belt and round her neck a thick gold chain

9

which Fâtima had given her, and which she wore
day and night. Her skin was not too wrinkled
for her age, her eyes magnificent, and sometimes
her rebellious little *hennéd* curls would come
peeping out from under her pink silk turban.
In the streets she wore a black satin tcharchaff
and was also well shod ; her manners were
aristocratic, and as she was generally somewhere
within calling distance of Fâtima, I supposed at
first she must be a relation.

One of my greatest difficulties in Turkey is to
be sure of the social standing of the men and
women. The man you might easily in my country
take for a groom is perhaps the Pasha's son ; the
man you might take for the Pasha's son is perhaps
a domestic. The woman seated in the place of
honour, dressed like a charwoman, may be the
mother of a great statesman or a minister's wife,
and amongst them all sits the old nourrice, one of
the family.

The nourrice's answer to my teasing was so
different from what I had expected that I did not take
her seriously till she began asking questions about
my country. "What did it matter after all,"
she concluded, " if the sun never shone ? " She
would be there to make the clove wine if Fâtima
coughed, and the coffee and the pilaff, too ; she
would be there to speak to Fâtima in the language
of their own native land, and above all to teach
the little girl to say her prayers. The one thing
which was worrying her, however, was her veil.

What would she do if the police tried to make her wear a hat? She never had worn one and she never would.

" But your husband," I ventured to suggest.

" Fâtima is my child," she answered, " I will choose him a suitable wife," and she seemed astonished that I should see anything extraordinary in the fact that a foster mother should follow her child even to the other end of the earth, if necessary, and relieve her conscience by seeing that her husband was properly cared for during her absence.

I asked Fâtima whether this situation was frequent in Turkey. " It does happen," she answered. Then she told me the curious life story of the golden-haired erstwhile beauty, who in the evening of her existence was allowed to occupy a modest place in the basement of our Konak in exchange for her occasional service as dish-washer. She had started her career as an oar maiden on the caique in which the Sultan Abdul-Aziz rowed about on the lake in his park when he was weary. But she grew tired of celibacy, asked to be allowed to marry, and finally was presented to an old Pasha as a reward for his distinguished services to the State.

When the Pasha died, she married a man years her junior, whom she loved with all her heart and soul, and who in his turn loved her. Knowing how bitterly disappointed he was not to have children, she herself found another wife for him, left for her successor everything she possessed, and came penniless to Fâtima. And her husband? When not washing dishes, she dreams of him as she wanders amongst the garden trees, she writes long letters to him which she never posts, and he, probably, has forgotten her very existence.

All these curious stories brought us back to the subject of polygamy, and the harem with two wives I wanted to visit.

" Do you know of a harem where there is more than one wife? " asked Fâtima.

" Yes ! " answered the nourrice, " my two friends, the wives of the Dervishe ' R.' "

The words " My two friends " surprised me just a little, but I made no comment. It was arranged, however, that I should go the next day to the dervishe service and *Sutanna* should take me afterwards to call on the two wives. *Sutanna* knew all the dervishes in the out-of-the-way districts of old Stamboul. These performances, I may at once explain, have little in common with the paid exhibitions arranged for tourists in Pera and Scutari. The Faithful howled and danced not for the curious spectators, for none were admitted, but to praise the Lord, the whole of their creed being based on the words of the Psalmist David : " Make a joyful noise unto the Lord, make a loud noise and sing praise."

On these occasions I accompanied *Sutanna* to the woman's gallery, always wearing a veil. Seated on a cushion I watched the worshippers

below through the lattice work of the gallery.
The atmosphere was never very invigorating, the
lack of fresh air being supplied by an unpleasant
mixture of incense, sandal wood, and tobacco, and
a stuffiness which almost choked me.   We were
so many women huddled together in this kind of
magnified dog-kennel, and the worshippers, too,
needed some space to do the same movements as
the male howlers in the body of the mosque
below.   The dancing dervishes were charming.
I enjoyed the weird piping of what sounded like
a shepherd's flute, the curious beating of the
drum, the graceful movements of the men as
they " waltzed " bare-foot on the polished boards,
their wide skirts expanding and contracting like
a well-chosen crescendo.   Curiously enough the
women did not attend or follow the " dancers "
with the same delight as the " howlers " ; they
preferred the noise.   What an extraordinary con-
ception must they not have had of the Deity, these
poor primitive souls, that they should suppose
He would find delight in the medley of grunt
and bark which accompanied their curious con-
tortions and drowned in its hideousness the
wonderful words " Allah al Ecbar." (God is
Great.)

I was studying the profile of the polygamous
dervishe who sat on his legs amongst the Faithful,
his arms crossed on his chest and his head reverently bowed.   He had a turned-up nose, on the
top of which rested a growth.   He certainly was

a hideous specimen of humanity, and yet two
women loved him!

Yes, after all, is not humanity the same all the
world over, Mahomet saw the danger of a priesthood, he did not wish the holy men to have more
power than, let us say, the recorder of the Quakers.
The Sheik-ul-Islam himself impressed upon me
that there were no priests in Islam, and yet here
face to face with the truth, are dervishes who have
grafted on to the bare spirituality of the religion
of Mahomet *credenda*, fanaticism and external
manifestations, just as the priesthood of the West
has done in a different manner from the religior
of Christ.

Every one of the dangers which Mahomet tried
to guard against in denying a priesthood to Islam
are in existence to-day. The words of the Prophet are interpreted in such a manner as to keep
the people in ignorance, and in spite of the
large sums of money left by the Faithful to pious
foundations for their enlightenment. Do not the
dervishes in the Tekhi live on the fat of the
land and enjoy all the privileges of the " cloth " ?
It makes one sore to think when money for
the regeneration of the country is so urgently
needed that a poor woman whose six sons fell in the
war gives her bed-cover to the National Defence,
all this money is lying there in so unproductive a
form. It surprised me rather that, when the
shoe pinched so hard, the Turkish Government
did not take a leaf out of France's book, and help

itself to some of these funds.   After all, however, they have acted wisely, for the money can now be used for National Education.

The dervishe's two wives came in towards the end of the ceremony.   Sutanna, after kissing them both, introduced me, and we were invited to coffee in the harem.   The first wife was a sickly looking, resigned creature, not very much older than her colleague, to whom she seemed quite attached ; indeed, her attitude towards her rival was rather that of a mother.   She was quite content to wear the old clothes, to do the work to be done, to wait on us, to give way in everything to the second wife, a well-built, healthy woman not without charm, and whom Allah had blessed, for she was to be a mother.

The first wife talked to Sutanna with delight about the expected new-comer, and alluded to it as " our child."

She worked at its layette, she spared its mother every fatigue, she seemed as enthusiastic as a mother whose daughter is expecting a child ; and yet, who knows the sorrow which may have been gnawing at her heart-strings ?

For she loved her Master ; she was proud of him.   Sutanna had her confidence and told me so, and it was she and Sutanna together who chose as her successor, a friend of their own.

Strange and inexplicable it all seemed, and not altogether pleasant.   " Our grandmothers," one woman explained to me, " submitted to this as

their written fate; they could not understand why
pride should not allow us to accept such a
degrading position."

The pride of the Turkish woman takes her
through an ocean of suffering.   Just as the woman
of the last generation accepted to remain with
a rival for the sake of her children, now the
woman of this generation is too proud to take
advantage of the protection the law gives her in
monetary assistance for the upbringing of her
children when she leaves her husband.   Personally, I know more than two women working against
terrible odds to pay for the children's education.
When I have suggested alimony, " Never!" they
answer.

They, however, like other women of Turkey,
will learn as the women of the West are learning,
that they must, as individuals, insist on their
rights for the benefit of the community, and reserve
their pride for something else.

CHAPTER XII

FARTHER AFIELD—THE PRIMITIVE PEOPLE

ALAS! I have stayed too long in the charming society of Fâtima. In my quiet Eastern existence I have not noticed the flight of time. I came for a week, and I have stayed over twelve. Soon, I believe, I should have taken Fâtima's advice to send for my mother and stay here altogether.

And now winter has come. In my own country I had mapped out quite a different programme for myself. Constantinople, after all, is not Turkey. To know Turkey I must go right into the homes of the people of Anatolia, and the thought of spending my days on horseback and my nights sometimes in the homes of the primitive Turks, sometimes under the starlit sky, with the glorious Eastern moon to kiss me to sleep, gave me courage to break away for a while from my matter-of-fact grinding existence of the West. But I have been so completely under the spell of my new life that I have not even known the day of the month. When writing one of my letters I remember

I questioned a friend as to the date. "Must
you really put the date?" she asked. "It isn't
a matter of life and death," I answered, "but one
generally does so in my country." "Well, my
dear," she went on, "you must wait till my husband returns, he, perhaps, will know; I haven't
the least idea."

Ah, happy country, where one can forget
even the date! Alas!—yes, I say alas!—its
hour has come. It, too, will have to take on
the uncomfortable yoke of civilization, and be
a plain, matter-of-fact people, like the rest of
Europe. I have felt all the while I stayed with
Fâtima as if I were present at a beautiful sunset,
and I must not lose the joy of drinking in
every ray of light, for in a few moments night
would be there. "How you notice every
detail," Fâtima said to me one day. "It is
all so beautiful," I replied, as I felt this was
the end of the true "East" in the old sense of
the word—the cook, who goes to sleep over his
work, and serves the meals according to the
sun, or a still more accurate timepiece—his own
healthy appetite; the coachman, whose two great
passions are his horses and the history of Turkey,
which he has acquired from conversation only,
since he can neither read nor write; Miss Chocolate, who in a month's time will take her place as
the wife of a coffee-skinned railway official. I
had the feeling when I left my dear Fâtima this
morning that when next I return to this country

this charming picture will have passed into
eternity.

And Fâtima herself! A true daughter of the
East, and proud to be so. Dear little friend,
with the blue-black hair, olive skin, and dark
eyes!—such a striking contrast to myself. How,
in the hurry and bustle of our life, I shall miss
her soft, low voice, and the gentle touch of her
hand, and the "Let us sit down quietly and
rest, and I will explain our Eastern customs to
you." I have been with Fâtima in the hardest
moments of her life. Where has that tiny little
creature found in these moments of anguish—
which would have crushed us Western women
used to the tumble and rough of life—a strength
of will to carry her dry-eyed through an ocean of
suffering? These Turks have the pride of Emperors. How we have misjudged them! When
the enemy was at their very door, when half their
Fatherland was gone, Europe noticed how they
listened to all the news with dry eyes and ap-
parently resigned indifference. But this is not
indifference—it is pride. When Fâtima was
mourning the loss of her little baby girl she told
me calmly her heart was broken, but never would
she let me see the tears which soaked her pillow
at night. Indifference, indeed! I never met
any one who cared less for her own woes and
more for the woes of others. Lady Mary
Montagu was right when she said, "There is
as much sense in asking the refugees of Greek-

street to write about the Court of St. James's as in asking the average woman to write about the women of Turkey."

And now, although winter is here, I have come as far as Broussa and the neighbouring villages to take a peep into the lives of these primitive people of Asia Minor. The sea has been rough for days; so rough that the cautious captain has preferred to remain quietly in the sheltered harbour. But to-day, one might almost imagine the hospitable Turks had ordered the Bosphorus to spread itself out into a blue satin carpet all along the way, and the sun to give a special performance in my honour.

A comfortable cabin is reserved for me. I am accompanied by one of the most eloquent orators of the Young Turk party, N—— Bey, who in his turn is accompanied by a secretary. This man is a patriot to the core; nothing counts with him but his Fatherland. He would be a gentleman even were he in rags, and if he had to assassinate an enemy of his beloved Fatherland, at least he would set about it like a gentleman. The boat we travelled on was named after a favourite Sultana. The first thing that greeted my eye was the notice, " Private cabin." Was everything on board, then, to be translated into English? My heart thumped with delight. Alas! things do not always go as quickly as one could wish, and the explanation of the English was nothing more poetical than the fact that the steamboat

which now bears the name of a much-loved
Sultana was a cast-off boat belonging to the
Brighton and South Coast Railway Company.

On the little stretch of railway which extends
from Modana to Broussa no one hurries. One
station is called " The Persians," and the next
" The Jews," and each time the train stops the
kindly guard gives the *souje* (water merchant) a
chance of doing some business before the train
moves on again. " If only you had come in the
spring," my companion tells me, as I give way to
the enthusiasm I feel for all I see around me,
" you, who love the flowers, what pleasure they
would give you ! " But I am content with small
mercies. Everything, after all, is relative in this
world. And when I think of London at this
moment, shrouded in fog, whilst we are surrounded
by a blue sky, a blue sea, trees in all their autumn
glory, and the air which caresses my face like *iced
velvet*, I am thankful for what Broussa can give
me at present.

We had a long, cold drive from the station,
but I do not mind this in the least, for the long
way takes me by the tomb of Kara Kheuz and
his partner, Hadgi Vadt. Two insignificant
turban-topped stones, which time has almost
laid horizontal, spring out of the bank on the
side of the road. One gets so used in Turkey
to seeing tombs springing out of places where
they are least expected that unless one's attention were particularly drawn to it one would

never have noticed this insignificant, neglected
burial-place of a great man. I say great man,
because I am told that it is from Kara Kheuz
that the great Molière took so much of his
inspiration, and his well-known *que fait-il dans
cette galère?* comes straight from this source.

In the inn where we are staying there is
no woman to attend to me. This does not
trouble me in the very least, and men, after
all, make excellent housemaids. They give me
cheese for breakfast, rustic bread, and coffee
à la turque, after which I rise early and dress,
in order to see all there is to be seen whilst the
daylight lasts. The inn is situated on a hill;
there are sulphur and Turkish baths attached
to it. Broussa is the happy possessor of
springs, which for a European *Kurort* would
be a fortune; but where is the European who
would come to a *kurort* without a casino? Our
inn is not in Broussa itself, but in the neighbouring village. Broussa lies at the foot of the
hill, bathed in a pale blue mist, which looks from
the distance like the sea, and there are lines of
naked poplar trees jutting out of the wide blue
expanse, and an horizon such as I love, for it
never seems to end.

S—— Bey, the sympathetic principal of the
Broussa Lycée for boys, is to be my guide whilst
I am here. My guide from Constantinople is
visiting his old friends, who are arranging a
meeting-lecture at the town hall, for never is

this charming politician allowed to leave a town
without first speaking to the people. A lecture
from N—— Bey! It is the event of the year!
There is nothing whatsoever going on here after
sunset. A handful of dimly lighted cafés, where
a few resigned-looking Turks sit sipping a
halfpenny cup of coffee, talking rarely, smoking
generally, and occasionally humming a favourite
ghazelle (a popular song which sounds to my
Western ear like a dirge). But when N—— Bey
speaks the cafés are deserted, and the proprietors
themselves are amongst the audience.

It was a splendid meeting. A seething mass
of 2,000 odd fezzes and turbans; old and young,
rich—or rather, shall we say, the better class—
and poor, workmen, hamals, and the Grand
Vizier's brother. The present Governor of Broussa,
who was himself absent, was represented. The prefect and his officials came to the big entrance door
to fetch me, and after a little speech of welcome
conducted me into the *mayoral* parlour, where
I drank coffee and syrup before the meeting
began. The prefect is one of those kind-faced
Orientals who belong to the Turkey which is
passing away. He has a little, withered-up,
dark-skinned face, and big, brown, wondering
eyes; he wears a long coat made of Persian
embroidery, and lined with fur, and a big turban,
which looks too heavy for his small head, and
although he is the municipal head of the ancient
capital of the Turks, he can neither read nor write.

And here, again, the inborn good manners of the Turks struck me. They had never before seen a woman at one of their meetings; they did not stare at me during the speech, they did not hang about the door to see the " curious monster" arrive and depart. When I took my seat beside the Prefect and his officials they rose respectfully; then I became one of themselves, and they paid no further attention to me.

I asked N——— Bey, when we travelled to Broussa, whether he prepared his speeches. " No," said he, " I speak from my heart." Although during the speech I understood no more than that his subject was the Fatherland, the sight of this man, who was ready to lay down his life for the Fatherland in danger, giving out the fire of his eloquence to stir the people to be ready, and this whole mass of people sobbing, moved me also to tears. That I should have wept without understanding a word sounds incomprehensible. I understood the sacred word " Fatherland." That was enough. Now should all Western critics who spoke of the Turkish " indifference" come and see these tears—tears of old men and boys. Where were the fathers of these youths and the sons of the old men? I asked. The answer I knew—they had fallen for the Fatherland.

N——— Bey, explaining the reasons for the Turkish losses, found three principal causes: First, the absence of the clergy, if the Moslem holy men can be called by that name. "Ever since the beginning of Islam," said he, "the clergy have been at the wars encouraging the soldiers when they grew faint-hearted, and helping to care for the sick. In this last war not one Hodja took part." Secondly, he blamed the dynasty for not sending one of its members to lead the troops. Before the reign of Abdul-Hamid the Kalife of Islam always led the troops; the dynasty, like the clergy, had forgotten its duty. The third cause found was that the people had not obeyed the dictates of civilization. That is true. But on whom can the blame be laid? On the shoulders of that fallen tyrant who is eking out his days in a prison-palace on the shores of the Bosphorus. It is when one goes about this country and sees the extraordinary ignorance of this people that one realizes something of the hideous crime of the Sovereign, who for thirty-three years terrorized his people, and the extraordinary courage of the Young Turks who deposed him.

Civilization the Turks must have. Much as I have loved the reposeful nature of the quiet cities of Islam, much as I feel the sight of electric light and gas and electric trams offends my artistic soul, I know only too well that Turkey must "move on with the centuries." And here again one recognizes the gigantic task the Young Turks have before them. Hamid is no longer on the throne, but Hamid's work lives on. You cannot repair in five years the damage of thirty-three. You cannot in five years change the character of a people used to a régime of terror. I see in the faces of these poor old men a resignation which is the result of a crushing and brutalizing tyranny; they are like horses which have taken fright. What can Young Turkey do with them? "You cannot put new wine into old bottles," says the Prophet of Nazareth. Young Turkey is wise in staking all its efforts on the coming generation, and giving power to a Minister not yet thirty years of age.

S—— Bey is determined I shall not leave Broussa till I have visited every stone it contains. It was the "woman's day" at the Turkish baths this morning, and I went into all the steaming heat to see the women of the people spending, as it were, a holiday. They can stay there all day for 2d. if they like; so they take their food, and their children, and their children's children, and make a day of it. Fat old ladies in gaudy-coloured tunics sit huddled up in corners singing contentedly, others walk about, dragging their clogs over the baking marble floors, whilst little girls and boys, with wine flasks tied round their waists in the place of lifebelts, swim about the fountains like little brown fishes.

We have been to the market-place and the old bazaar, which very much resembles the bazaar of Stamboul, except that one has Moslem merchants to deal with instead of Levantine Christians.

What a charming difference! Yes, but these good-mannered men will never make successful merchants. I buy a piece of embroidery. " The price," says the merchant, "is 12 francs.—2*d*. profit for me," he adds. I offer 10*s*. for a blue stone. " I could not take more than 6*d*.," says the merchant; " it is only glass."

I want to buy a couple of the charming blue bead necklaces which every quadruped here wears round his neck. It does not matter really whether his harness is worn almost to a thread, no harm can come to him if he has the bead necklaces round his neck. " This lady loves your country," S—— Bey tells the merchant, and the merchant will not take a penny for his wares. I go to see the Broussa silks. " Is this the lady who loves my country?" asks the merchant. A pink silk dress is mine, but all attempts to get the bill have been in vain.

And, at the bazaar at Stamboul, who has not experienced the disagreeable bartering which takes place between the merchant and the customer? I went one day with Fâtima. The man tried to sell us imitation antique embroideries for the price of real antiques. Fortunately, Fâtima knew the difference, for I did not. Then the merchant showed us the real article. " Very beautiful," commented he; "a beautiful price!" replied Fâtima. " But I never cheat Turks," although he had tried, he assured us, "only English people," for, naturally, he did not recognise through the

thick veil I was wearing the features of a woman
of that race " he always cheated when he could."

The women in the villages here are not veiled,
as are the women of Constantinople. Their hair
and shoulders are covered with yellow embroideries, of which I was given a sample, and they
sit astride their ponies, mules, or donkeys, as the
case may be, often without saddles, and a well-
worn cord only as bridle and reins. They carry
a rather substantial twig of a tree for a whip,
which they hold threateningly before the donkey's
eyes whilst mounting, but I never saw them
use it.

Horseback, of course, is the only way of getting
about this country. The horses are sure-footed,
if not very active, and at each village travellers
find a fairly steady pole, to which a horse is
tied up and left. The kindly villagers feed
him and water the horse, and the little, panta-
looned children play with his tail and stroke his
body—he is quite resigned. We rode over to
Hamidlair, a village about two and a half hours
away. On the verandah of the schoolhouse was
placed a chair for me, which had been procured
with very great difficulty. The schoolhouse itself
could accommodate twenty children, ten little boys
on one side, and ten little girls on the other, and
the schoolmaster stands between the children and
addresses first one sex and then the other. He,
too, is a picturesque person, with the honest
Eastern face and big, brown eyes. He wears

a turban and long, brown coat. The schoolmaster's salary is paid in corn, which means, of
course, when the harvest is good, salary is high,
and vice versa. It seems extraordinary to think
that in this enlightened twentieth century wages
can still be paid in corn.

I went to visit the wife of the schoolmaster.
She lived in a two-storeyed house of four rooms,
with a tiny garden, where a cow, a goat, and
a lamb had space to walk about and remain great
friends. The young wife was about seventeen,
and lived with her mother and grandmother and
little baby. They all came to the door to meet
me, and, kissing the hem of my dress, they led
me by the hand up a wooden staircase ladder to a
room which was furnished with cushions all round
—their chairs by day and their beds by night.
The bare boards were scrupulously clean, and the
cushions a welcome resting-place for my tired
limbs. I wanted to take off my boots, like the other
women, but my hostess refused to allow me. After
having tucked me up amongst the cushions, with
a queenly gesture she took off her ear-rings, her
ring, and a jade bracelet, and gave them to me,
but I naturally declined to accept them. This
jewellery, together with a new pair of clove-ball
silk pantaloons, were all the worldly goods this
woman possessed, and she was ready to give them
all to me, a stranger. Then the grandmother
came, bringing for me a cup of milk warm from
the goat, and the great-grandmother put in as a

token of respect for the honoured guest seven lumps of sugar.   And I had to drink it!

I loved being among that primitive household. They had bread to eat and milk to drink ; their own vegetables they grew in the little patch of garden, where the animals walked about at leisure, but they never ate meat, nor did they feel the want of it—to have told them they were poor would have surprised them.

CHAPTER XIII

THE PULSE OF THE NATION

A EUROPEAN official, who has lived here all his life (and he is an old man now), is astonished at my recklessness in trusting myself as I have done to the protection of the "unspeakable" Turks. He was born and bred with the idea that Turks were "unspeakable," and consequently has nothing to do with them, unless he can possibly help it, and when he does he lets them see he dislikes them. Extraordinary it is, that there should be Europeans in this country who, after living almost a lifetime amongst a people, have not got to know them one little bit better! They make their whole existence, as it were, an island—their thoughts, their actions, their words, even their friends—and fondly imagine themselves to be patriots. "How uncomfortable! How nasty! Oh! I wouldn't like that!" they exclaim, as I describe to them some of the customs of this people amongst whom they have lived over fifty years. "Whatever did you do in a household where there were no forks and knives?" The answer is not very difficult to guess; but they

seem incapable of understanding my delight at
eating with my fingers, like the primitive people
who entertained me.

And yet, after only a short time, how different
is my experience of these same " unspeakable "
Turks ! Every day since I have been here some
woman comes with a present for me ! I have
received a wooden spoon, stuffs, embroideries,
Brussels sprouts, melons, sweetmeats, yourout
(curdled milk), and one poor woman has walked
from a neighbouring village, bringing me a little
lamb; I have explained to her, however, that
although I much appreciate her gift, the fog of
London would kill the little thing, and he had
better, therefore, remain where he is in the sun.
And why have all these women come bringing
me presents ? Simply out of gratitude (and
gratitude is one of their chief characteristics) to a
woman who loves their country, and because that
woman is English.

Right into the very heart of Asia the word
" England " stands for something almost super-
human. "We can never, never forget that
England has shed her blood for us," said one
day the Turkish Heir to the throne. England
stands for all that is good and honest and just.
England is the fairy godmother, who, with a
touch of her magic wand, could put everything
straight for them. In the families where there
are two governesses, an Englishwoman and a
Frenchwoman, it is the Englishwoman who is

given the position of trust, the Englishwoman who sleeps in the children's room, the English-woman who buys their clothes ; in short, whatever the mother cannot do herself she prefers the Englishwoman to do for her. "The English-woman told me so, therefore I believe her," is a phrase which I myself have heard ; and one mother, quite recently, who was, in spite of my presence, weeping bitterly because her son had gone to Paris to study, added, "It would have all been so different had he gone to England." My host tells me, too, that when he was a little boy, and the Circassians were groaning under the Russian yoke, his mother and her friends used to comfort each other with the hope that the English most surely would come to deliver them. They did not think of the Turks, who were their natural deliverers, and who at that time were quite strong enough to come to their assistance ; but their thoughts always turned to the great far-away England, who always came to help States in bondage, or States struggling for regeneration.

And so, when I think of this great prestige of my country, it seems a thousand pities that there are persons doing their best to destroy that prestige.

I hear the Turks called suspicious—during the reign of Abdul Hamid, perhaps, yes—they had every reason for being so. I have trusted them, and they of all the nations of Europe have never given me the wrong change.

I have trusted them, and they have not deceived
me. One day, I remember, I had to cross the
bridge without Fâtima, and pay my own toll.
Not knowing the Turkish for what I wanted to
say, I opened my purse, and the man took out
what he wanted and put back the change. My
boxes have never been locked since I left the
boat. When I return from my afternoon drive
Miss Chocolate takes off my " tcharchaff" and
puts away my purse. My books, my papers, my
letters are all open ; the few jewels I possess are
on my table. I close my eyes in the homes of
these humble villagers confident that no harm
will come to me ; that they will not unfasten my
pearls whilst I sleep. In our Western countries
should I not be scolded for putting temptation in
their way ? And I, in my turn, feel sure they
trust me.

My friend Zeyneb lives at No. 43. It is a
luxury to have a number. Addresses are generally given in this manner : the district first, let
us say " Kiz Tach," for example ; then, as further
direction, "the house at the corner, near the
fountain, near the convent, near the mosque."
One generally trusts to Providence, in the form
of a kindly stranger, to find the way, and I
must say they take unending pains to help one.
With a number, then, I say to myself, it will
be easy to find Zeyneb. But alas, there are
other No. 43's in the district, these numbers,
for the most part, having been purchased at

the bazaar and put on the door without rhyme
or reason, and as a sort of decoration.   To find
my friend's house, which is ten minutes' walk
from Pera, it took my coachman two and a half
hours and cost me 2of., and " the way is so easy,"
explained Zeyneb.   After that I walked, following
these instructions : " Always keep on the cobbles
which lie on the earth from north to south.
Although the road may turn and twist, mount and
descend, as long as you keep on the north to
south lying cobbles you will be all right."   And
after dark, when I have taken that way, had the
Turks been suspicious, what would they not have
imagined I was doing when suddenly, from my
little bag, I extracted a box of matches and
examined the cobbles to be sure I had not strayed
on to those lying from east to west.   Once or
twice a kindly old man brought his lantern, and
came with me as far as the hillock, at the side of
which Zeyneb's No. 43 is situated.

When I remarked on the number of maps and
the prominence given to drawing of maps in the
Turkish schools, my guide answered, " You
English on your comfortable island do not require
to know the map of Europe."

Yes, a thousand pities it is that we all of us,
from the highest of the land to the schoolboy,
should not have a more accurate knowledge of
the map of Europe and a more accurate knowledge of the peoples on that map.   If all those
who are now working in the cause of peace

turned their efforts towards making the nations
of a country understand one another better war
would be much less possible. If only we had
more knowledge of the people of other lands,
many diplomatic errors could be avoided. Over
and over again we have slighted the Moslems
of our Empire. How many of us even realize
that King George rules over more Moslems than
any other sovereign. Hear the asinine remarks
of our young subalterns about the uncivilized
Indian *niggers* who must be kept in their place!!"
How dare they thus humiliate persons of a
civilization older and greater than our own.

There is a wonderful brotherhood amongst the
Moslems. Any injustice to their Moslem brothers
of Turkey is counted as an insult to Moslem
Indians ; they have written so to me. Unfortunately we have not this same brotherhood
amongst us Christians. I have in my possession
a letter written by a Lazarist Father, deploring
the possibility that Constantinople might fall into
the hands of the Greeks. "They are waging
war," he says, "in the name of the Cross, but
does Europe not know that that Cross is *tout ce
qu'il a de plus Grecque*" (sic). What a splendid
example of Christian brotherhood to show to the
Moslems of the world! He prefers the *infidel*
Turk to another member of the Christian Church
because the Turk has offered him hospitality and
allowed him to have his churches and his missions,
and has in no way interfered with his religious

liberties, whereas from his brother Christian he could not expect such broad-mindedness. And what horrors would not have been committed at the Holy Sepulchre had not the Turks been there to guard it against the Christians. Sad, indeed, it is that this wonderful Christian religion of ours should be divided against itself to the detriment of its best interests.

Had the Bulgarians and the Christian natives of the Balkans gone out to wage war like Hottentots, or any of the other nations they have the impertinence to regard as savages, we might have pitied them; but that they should carry the Cross, and wage war in the name of the Cross, what Christian can ever forgive them? "We used to respect your Christian Cross," one day a Turk said to me; "we used to bow respectfully when the Cross passed in the streets, but the Bulgarians have dragged that Cross in the mire." I was one day reading with a friend the beautiful, wonderful story of Jesus of Nazareth.

"This is not the Christ of the Bulgarians," she said. "No, indeed," I replied.

.   .   .   .   .

And Young Turkey—has she yet had a chance? We cannot pass judgment on them till they have had ten years' fair trial. Unfortunately for them, their revolution was a little too idealistic. Theirs was to be a bloodless revolution! Bloodless revolution it was, and it astonished the whole civilized world. Alas! they have now to learn

you cannot make a revolution without shedding
blood, any more than a doctor can amputate a
limb without shedding blood.   The poison they
should have cleared away at the time of their
revolution they have to clear away now; the
minions of Hamid, who earned a substantial living
as spies, are still there to plot and plan for the
return of the tyrant.

The Young Turks have had to pay a heavy price
for their experience! Counter-revolutions and in-
surrections to the number of seven, and three European wars, and the last two against five nations!
Add to this also, the humiliating interference of
Europe. I have seen here households with a Greek
cook, an Armenian *bonne à tout faire*, an Albanian
cavass, and a Turkish gardener.   It is no easy
matter to rule such a household.   See what tact
and patience it requires. The Armenian, for some
reason, insults the cook, who replies by throwing
the chicken at her head; then the Albanian and
the Turk are dragged into the quarrel, and you
hear them cursing one another in their different
languages.   Who does not pity the mistress of a
house like this?   Who is the person so tactless as to
interfere?   And is it not the same with the Turkish
Government, except that they have the Syrians
and Arabs as well?   When things seem to be
going on fairly smoothly, the Powers, with bung-
ling, interfering hands, come along and " demand
reforms."   " We cannot make headway with
our reforms," writes my compatriot from Trebi-

zonde; "some Power always objects to something."
And what will the Power say now, when I tell
them that here in the schools of Asia Minor the
walls are covered with German maps, the apparatus
in the agricultural college in German, and most
of the scientific instruments are German? Poor
Turkey, will she ever have a soul to call her own?

.   .   .   .   .

Unfortunately, the world always seems to forget that the key to the understanding of a nation
is in the hands of the women.   One sex cannot
achieve true greatness without the assistance of
the other.   "If I only had a woman who could
tell me what to do and say just at the right
moment," a Turk said to me one day.   How
well I understand what he felt.   Where would
our political men be without their womenkind,
not only to tell them what to do and say, but often
to do and say it for them?   This Turk in question
had made a social mistake; he told me all about
it.   In my country a charming wife's smile can
atone for multitudes of social sins much more
serious; but here——.   Political men cannot be
expected to bear on their shoulders both burdens
political and burdens social.

I have been, whilst here, to see the Governor's
wife.   She is a sister of the Khedive, and her
husband a brother of the Grand Vizier, and, like
his brother, he receives no salary for his services.
This beautiful and accomplished lady, who dresses
only in Turkish dresses, made of Turkish stuffs,

whose very jewels are all set, not in Paris, but in the old Arabian Fâtima style—see of what assistance she could be to her husband if she took her place at the head of his table, as our Western women do! The Princess, who speaks five Western and three Oriental languages, has read, perhaps, more than most of her countrywomen (she is Egyptian), and she has supplemented her knowledge by travelling, not only in every European country with the exception of Russia, but right across to San Francisco and back through Canada, "and you see," she added, charmingly, "I can give all my attention to travelling because I have no dressmaker worries."

The man who has not beside him some woman who can judge instinctively for him, and whisper "Beware!" from the bottom of my heart I pity. him. How many men can tell at a glance whether another is a gentleman or not? A woman generally can, a man sometimes. I have seen most charming Turks with friends unworthy of them. "Surely," I have said to myself, "you would not have made a friend of such a man had your wife been there to guide you!" And so, in trying to solve the riddle of the Turk the answer is to be found behind that harem door. Both men and women blame the harem, and rightly so, for most of their disasters ; the remedy they see in the education of the women.

I have come to Turkey at indeed an interesting

time. Here in Broussa I have not marvelled, as
did the Oxford professor of Arabic, in the visitors'
book, about the boys' knowledge of that language.
I have congratulated them on their first football
match. I have admired the children's first attempts
at plain needlework (not embroidery, that is born
in them), dancing, singing, and drawing. In
all these arts they have made progress, and
although the art students' trees are a little bald
and a little too green, and their cows' eyes a
little too near their tails, there is in that work
a great promise of better.

The Belgian head-mistress of the School of
Arts and Crafts, at the opening of which I was
present, and who has allowed me to go so often
to see the working of a school which, naturally,
interests me, tells me, " double the number of
children have arrived over the number for whom the
Government provided accommodation," and she
added, " We must just put up with the discomfort.
They are like hungry children asking for bread,
and I dare not turn them away."

And now Turkey is to find teachers of her own
to instruct all these children. She cannot always
be asking the assistance of the foreigner. She
knows to her cost now what that means, and we
who wish her well will leave no stone unturned to
help her to help herself—to improve the teachers'
training college, and assist some of the most
brilliant pupils to have the benefit of English and
French methods of organisation.

11

CHAPTER XIV

FORBIDDEN GROUND—THE HOLY TOMB

I HAVE been with Fâtima to the Holy Tomb of Eyoub. Ever since I came here I have looked forward to this experience ; not so much, let me confess at once, to see the beautiful porcelains which cover its sacred and historic walls as to contradict the regulation which reserves entrance to the Holy Tomb exclusively for "believers."

This was not my first visit to Eyoub. Five years ago I had the humiliating experience of being refused admission to the tomb because I was wearing a hat; now I am wearing a veil who can tell whether I am Moslem or Christian ? Last time I came to Eyoub in a friend's launch. It had been freshly painted, and was out that day as it were for its maiden trip. We had chosen an afternoon when the sea was calm and the atmosphere clear enough to enjoy the magnificent view one has of the opposite shore, and all the hieroglyphics and brass-work on the launch were dancing in the sunshine like little golden butter-flies.

Although we could not visit the mosque that

afternoon five years ago, we did not give to the tombs and the curious cemetery the time they deserved. We climbed up the steep and stony path which leads to a " Well of Souls," where a witch with wonderful powers of divination can not only predict what will happen in the future, but will tell you the valuables stolen during the year and in the water of the well the faces of the thieves can be distinctly seen. But we never found the witch.

And now, since my last visit, Eyoub does not seem in the least bit changed. There is the same merchant who sells you corn with which to feed the pigeons, there are the same devout-looking turban-headed inhabitants, the same thickly veiled women, the same unending streams of beggar children, and I even think I can recognise our boatman of five years ago. He is still a little on my conscience. The launch, I remember, was too big to land at Eyoub, so a caïque was called and we were rowed up to the little landing-place ; and I remember so distinctly the boatman was not paid. When we returned, however, he was either praying or had gone home to rest. Calling another man, we engaged him to row us to the launch ; he was paid and given the money for his colleague. With Western *naïveté*, I asked whether the first boatman would ever receive his money. " Why, of course," answered my friend, not in the least understanding my question.

We drove to Eyoub this time. A long, de- lightful drive it was through the picturesque

quarters of Stamboul, which are now becoming so
familiar to me and to which I have become so
attached. The market-place with its richly coloured
fruits; the well-balanced shops of meat, bread,
and other wares so charmingly arranged on the
mule's back—I watch them almost as one watches
by the death-bed of a loved one. Like death,
the passing of the primitive Turk is inevitable;
but that does not make his going any the less
sad, nor does it prevent one's mourning. . . .

It was Friday afternoon. The Faithful were at
prayer when we arrived. I wanted to see the
mosque; but how could I, even as a veiled
woman, take my place amongst the women?
Much as I admire the wonderful solemnity of the
Eastern prayers—much as I, a Christian, would
have loved to worship Allah with my Moslem
sisters—I was just a little frightened; my action
might be mistaken for irreverence.

We went, however, into the gallery reserved for
the Sultan, and through the lattice-work windows
we had a good view of the mosque below. But
the mosque and its historic contents—for it is in
this mosque that the Sultan is girt with the sword
of Islam—were dwarfed to me in the magnificence
of seeing men and women in one mass bending
in rhythmic supplication to the God of us all.
The women were screened off from the men, but
they were "believers," every one of them, and
they worshipped with a reverence I had never
yet seen elsewhere.

Of its charity, one branch of our Christian Church prays every Sabbath for Turks and heretics. There are some heretics I know who resent being classed with the Turks. I am proud to be classed with the Turks; but then, I am a heretic who has seen them at prayer. . . .

      .   .   .   .   .

Eyoub-Ansari-Khalid-ben-Said, to give him his full title, was a favourite standard-bearer of the Prophet, and during the siege of Constantinople he fell. About eight centuries after his death a body was exhumed which was supposed to be his, and was buried by Mahomet the conqueror, who placed it with pomp and ceremony beside the sword of the Prophet. To his tomb come pilgrims who have special favours to ask the saint, and he has accomplished, I am told, some marvellous cures. It was not a little surprising to me that these superstitions had also crept into Islam—yet who would grudge the ignorant the comfort of their beliefs?

      .   .   .   .   .

Slowly and reverently I followed Fâtima and her friend across the wide courtyard, whose plantain tree stretched like a magnificent green canopy between us and the sky; a flight of white pigeons flew out to greet us. "Only do not speak!" warned Fâtima once again as we crossed another courtyard to the entrance of the Holy Tomb On arriving at the mausoleum, we took off our

shoes and left them on the doorstep. The
thought did just flash through my mind that it
would be rather uncomfortable should a passer-by
take a fancy to my new shoes; but I soon felt
ashamed of my Western suspicions—and, after
all, I have left my shoes so often outside mosques
and never have they been taken. . . .

Fâtima and I have visited many tombs now.
They seem, these *turbés*, to reconcile one with
the idea of death, although it is only the great
of the land whose mortal remains are kept in
a mausoleum. In a coffin covered by a shawl and
surrounded by candles, with his Koran and other
precious souvenirs kept by his side ready for use,
the dead man rests—it is as if he were asleep, and
the guardian, who with his little *ménage* of beads
and cushions and a Koran, watches and tends
and shields him from all harm. These *turbés*
are not altogether what one would expect, however, in democratic Turkey. I should have fancied
that the equality preached in life would have
been enforced after death, and that the Turks
would have buried their dead in much the same
way as the Moravians, whose cemetery is the
picturesque lesson in Socialism which greets
me every morning from my study window in
Chelsea. Flat stone slabs level with the earth—
hidden at certain seasons of the year by long
grass, poppies, and cornflowers—whatever they
have been in life, on their long last journey they
start in the same vehicle.

The guardians of the tombs were generally men of learning—Hodjas, or at least students, who in the evening of their existence were content to guard the mortal remains of some great man.

There is a sympathetic and interesting old Hodja who guards the tomb of the Sultan Fathij, the Conqueror. His age in Biblical parlance is five score and ten, I am told, but I cannot vouch for the truth of this statement, since I have not seen his birth certificate. He is in perfect possession of all his faculties, walks, however, with difficulty, and he remains all day seated cross-legged on his cushions with his chaplet of amber beads and open Koran before him.

When we had removed our shoes, we sat down beside the old Hodja, and kissing his bony old hand as a sign of respect for his age and his office, Fâtima spoke to him of many things. " Tell him," I said, " that I am a Giaour." Fâtima did as I requested. " There are no Giaours in our religion," replied this kindly old man ; " every creature whom God has created is dear to Him and dear to us all."

" There are no Giaours in our religion." The answer was so unexpected and so splendid that I have repeated it to many who have attacked in my presence the fanaticism of Islam. Yet, was the old Hodja right after all ? Should he not rather have said, " There ought to be no Giaours in our religion " ? The Koran says in this respect, " We believe in God and what has

been sent down to us through the Holy Prophets
—we make no difference between them, and to
Him are we resigned." This being the case,
why then must I, a Christian, go to the Holy Tomb
disguised as a Mahometan?

The tomb of Eyoub was by no means the most
beautiful that I have seen in Turkey, nor the
most interesting. One had not time during one's
short stay to examine at leisure the porcelains.
But can they be compared in any way, I ask
myself, with the exquisite porcelains of the
Rustem Pasha mosque, that tiny, almost unknown
mosque to which one drives through the most
unappetising of the Stamboul streets, and whose
beauty so many tourists take for granted, since
the mosque is so difficult to find? Two or three
walks round the tomb, two or three peeps at
the silverwork, two or three glances at the purple
silk curtains, and we are out and have put on
our shoes again. Yes, indeed, one could see many
things more beautiful, but this tomb is beautiful
because of the difficulty in seeing it. To run
the risk once more of being torn to pieces by
an angry mob, as I did in Bosnia! Truly the
forbidden fruit is sweet indeed!

We walked slowly up the hills, threading our
way amongst the tombs; the wistaria was
shrivelling in the brownness of death, but there
was a wealth of those bright pink roses which
I had searched for in Zeyneb's garden in order
to make the rose jam. The ragged beggar

children follow us asking for alms. We pause and look towards the Golden Horn. How magnificent it all looks from here. There the five hills, each crowned by a mosque—Sud-ludgi, Piri Pasha, Hass-Kerin, Kassim Pasha, and Galata—can be seen as distinct as the five fingers of your hand, and all bathed in those wonderful uncertain and poetical tints which do not belong to our Western world.

One wanders on for a while, and then pauses to drink in just a little more of the beautiful landscape. Neither of us care to speak. We understand each other. A melancholy happiness, a calm, quiet feeling of resignation has taken possession of us, and in this resignation lies the whole enchantment of the East.

.   .   .   .   .

Just before we reached our carriage I saw a dear friend with her accustomed unselfishness escorting some English visitors round as much as they, Christians, could see of the holy city of Eyoub. She recognised my voice, and I was introduced as a Turkish lady to my compatriots.

I felt just a little guilty at their delight in meeting a real Turkish woman, but it was too dangerous to undeceive them in those fanatical surroundings. " And how well you speak English, too !" they said. " English was the first language I spoke," I answered truthfully. I wonder whether Miss A. ever told them who I really was.

CHAPTER XV

ON THE SHORES OF THE UPPER
BOSPHORUS

TO-DAY the sun peeping through the latticed windows of the harem has found me sleeping soundly on a comfortable mattress in the corner of my hostess's bedroom.

This is my first experience of Turkish country-house life, and it is so different to anything I have lived before—quaint, strange, charming, and at times confusing.

The house is immense—in most countries it would have been classed amongst the palaces—and it looks much larger than it really is, so scantily is it furnished.

But what a curious feeling of loneliness and desolation one has on first entering this house. What has happened to the poor place? Has it been successfully burgled? Have its inhabitants deserted it, or have they simply sent the best of the furniture to the emporium and the "household gods" to the bank? No pictures on the walls, no cosy corners, not even the elements of comfort. Then all of a sudden one discovers a table, almost hidden from view, covered with a host of tiny little articles, some of gold studded with precious stones, and the tinier they are the more they are cherished, and not one Turkish woman would change her table of useless nothings for a whole room full of Western comforts.

A large retinue of slaves and servants, many born on the premises, are supposed to keep the house in order, yet if every one of them looked "work" seriously in the face, three times their number would not suffice to do the work as we in the West would have it done.

But then, after all, we are not dealing with the West. The Turkish point of view is this : What a lot of fine tears and good worry are wasted in the West. Why should these Europeans criticise us ? Our beds do get rolled up and put away before it is time to take them out again. If there is a slight error of an hour on the wrong side of our mealtimes, we do get them. Should our rooms not be dusted daily, a friendly wind from the Bosphorus blows through and shifts the accumulation from place to place. And, says the Turkish woman, " I came to the country to rest. It may seem like running away from rest in order to rest, but that's my business. My household runs on the basis of good, delicious, creamy Turkish coffee at all hours of the day; everything else is in proportion."

The lord and master of the establishment is away. I do not know whether I am sorry. I

find Turkish men so much less interesting than
the women.   He, the master, will be back some
time within the *radius* of a month, and no one
ever supposes that my " week-end " will not have
extended long past that date.   For an unattached
woman to suggest that she deliberately wishes to
leave a friend's house without a serious reason for
doing so is an insult to a dear friend, and it
cannot be done.

.   .   .   .   .

Here in the country we are wearing Turkish
dresses—nice, comfortable dressing-gown arrange-
ments of Broussa silk, with wide sashes which
begin under our arms.   Mine has round the neck
and sleeves a fine, magnificent embroidery quite
out of proportion in value to the stuff to which it
is attached, that being the case with so many
Turkish embroideries.   I'm not sure that my
gown suits me, but that is a detail ; it was built
to accommodate a person twice my width and
half my height.   Only the master's slippers will
fit me, and the noise I make as I slither along the
wide hall in my silk gown is like that of a sail in
the river breeze.
We have done away, also, with our Western
coiffures, and it's a delightful change to be wearing
" flapper " plaits again, and so good for the hair.
And then, since the master is away, provided I
do not again commit the indecency of letting the
gardener see my hair and the sun kiss my

unveiled head, it matters little whether my hair is up or down.

The old *nourrice* having fallen out with both her shoes and stockings, has discarded them for the time being. Fortunately for her the rooms are carpeted. Taqui, the Armenian servant, who waits at table and is chief of the bed-distributing servants, has done away with her shoes ; to her heelless and toeless stockings, however, she has become so attached that no promise of better seems to tempt her away from the affection she feels for her old friends.

Amongst the staff there are two grooms and a coachman, relics of the " fat " years that are no more ; and although there are no horses in the stables, they still remain in the family, performing odd jobs like opening and shutting the huge windows at the back of the house.

In honour of my arrival, a tiny slave, perched like a fly on the top of a garden ladder, is busy cleaning the big window with a dainty silk handkerchief. She has been working for an hour, and although during that time she has toiled and accomplished little, and finally given up in despair, a small bright and shining place, sparkling in the sun, is there as proof of her charming compliment to the housekeeping qualities of my nation.

At the same time, one of my hostesses, seized with a fit of Western energy, is, with the assistance of a small camel's-hair brush and a box of water colours, busy supplying vivid red and green

parrots with those beaks and feathers which a
recent rainstorm has swept into air.

I suggest that if a brush can be found for me—
or a blunt knife—I would like to help in re-beaking
the parrots, or if anything from a pocket handkerchief to a towel can be found, I too might make
a shining place on the window-pane (how delightfully Turkish). But no—I am the honoured guest
—cigarettes, coffee, and sweets are provided for
me. I must remain in the seat of honour, as
far from the door as possible and right in the
draught of the gilded windows.

What a curious household we are! I have
obeyed my hostess's orders and brought no
luggage except a tooth brush. With everything
I have been provided, including my dresses, and
a *sachet* of linen is placed every night at the foot
of my mattress.

There is in my room a little *coiffeuse* which
looks like a doll's table in the emptiness of the
room ; a big armchair and a carpet complete the
furniture. We wash all together at a marble fountain, and when the weather is dry it takes an
eternity to wash, for the drainage is primitive
and you can only coax the drops of water out of
the tap at the rate of two a minute.

But oh! the silence and loneliness of my bedroom. It frightens me. I wish one of my friends
had offered to share it with me. I wonder how
long the sturdy candle will last! What a distressing shadow the *coiffeuse* makes on the

wall! There are little draughts coming from everywhere. The door, bereft of its handle, is attached by a string to a substantial nail and the window will neither open nor will it quite shut.

I sink down on to my mattress and fall asleep, but only to wake with a start a few moments later. Having reassured myself that the door is securely hooked on to the nail, I go back to my mattress again, but not for long : the moonbeams forcing their way through the latticed windows have given birth to all kinds of curious shadows, the *coiffeuse* is dancing in the candle light, and the deadly solemn silence is unearthly. If only the trees would shiver as I am shivering! If only a dog would bark! If only I could sleep! but paradox of paradoxes, it is the silence that is keeping me awake. "Yet I am not afraid," I say to myself. "I will sing to contradict this awful silence." I try, but not one note will come, for terror has frozen my voice to my throat.

Summoning up the little will-power that the soul-crushing harem life has left me, I stagger to the mirror to see how I look—but the horror of it! Can that hideous, unearthly face be mine? Where am I? and where am I going? My whole being is numbed, my ears are singing— I can remember no more. . . .

Exactly how I and my bed were transplanted to my friend's room I cannot tell. Did I faint? It is not a pleasant memory, nor one on which I care to dwell; let me turn my thoughts rather from my lonely bedroom to my curious bed—my beautiful, comfortable, unpractical bed.

The costliest of linen, the finest embroidery, a satin bolster allowed to show itself at both ends through the embroidery, satin cushions heavily embroidered with gold—the sheets sewn to the quilt—the gold itself worth a nice little sum— this is my bed, and all this magnificence cast down in the corner of an almost unfurnished room!

.   .   .   .   .

The day is breaking; the Bosphorus, so near to our window, is licking the steps of the rickety landing stage.   In a short while the little white boat will come paddling along, if it has pleased the captain to start at all, for unless the Bosphorus is calm he prefers not to run the risk of attaching his little boat to the landing stages which dance on the waves with more zest than his boat.

To-day the Bosphorus is calm.   The rising sun has thrown himself on its bosom, and their joyful union sheds around an indescribable happiness.   Who could imagine that only a week before, this peaceful resigned-looking river had raged and stormed and invaded the peaceful resigned souls who dwell so confidently near its banks?   But nothing will cure these unprepared Turks!   Over and over again the Bosphorus has overstepped its boundaries, swept away landing stages, entered the houses and caused damage irreparable—it is not natural for a river which looks so fine when it is sparkling in the sunshine to scowl and frown and storm, and no doubt each time it misbehaves they hope it will be the last. It is the character of the Turk, and so it will be always. Armenians—Greeks—Bulgarians—Germans will overstep his boundaries until they have swept him out of his harem and out of his land.

.   .   .   .   .

My hostess is stirring. How peacefully she sleeps, and how well her dark skin looks beside her scarlet cushions. She rushes to the window. She, too, will admire the Bosphorus.

"Beautiful, beautiful river," she says, half musing. "What would lonely Turkish women do without you to love!"

"Do you never tire of the Bosphorus?" I asked.

"Never," she answered; "everywhere I go I see it; it is my fixed standard for all comparisons of beauty in nature. When we are unhappy, or think we are unhappy, we throw our woes on to the Bosphorus and dream them away . . . what a consolation to follow even in imagination a barque that is slowly sailing away somewhere . . . perhaps to eternity."

But I am ravenous. My long, curious, eventful night has begotten for me the appetite of a wolf. I hope something will be given me to eat and drink without unnecessary delay. "Taqui," I call, for just as I was about to ask for something to eat she pops her head inside

12

the door without knocking, as is the custom. She kisses and hugs us both. Her hair, like ours, is done up into a hundred little plaitlets, and covered with a handkerchief—this method of wearing one's hair during the night has been advised by all the potentates of the witchcraft sisterhood. Turkish women have thick glossy hair—it is the result that counts.

Taqui has made the tea and is pouring it into a thin egg-shell porcelain cup. But it is not the same as when the *Hanoum* herself makes it. What can have happened? Nothing very serious, dear Taqui, except that you have forgotten to put in the tea. So tiny an error can easily be remedied and the water is quite respectably hot.

In the meanwhile there is enough food for me to go on with. A massive silver tray resting on an unsteady table is covered with all kinds of good things, but what shall I choose?

Fig compôte bathed and saturated in sugary juice. I cannot swallow it. Marrow jam equally saturated in sugar, sweet almond biscuits, brown sausages—(are they shrivelled up from age or is that their natural condition?)—there is also cheese with an equal proportion of sugar and more biscuits that probably have seen better days. . . . I have postponed my hunger.

Taqui has found the tea—a quarter-pound packet which, like the biscuits, looks as though it had seen better days. She is to make the tea; I, as the honoured guest, cannot offer to help. Pausing only to kiss the back of my neck, which she does whenever an occasion presents itself (and particularly at table when she is serving a dish floating in oil), Taqui shoots half the remaining tea out of the packet on to the lukewarm water . . . and waits to see me drink the unhappy result—it has not even been stirred. . . . Blessed is she who expecteth less than a good cup of tea on the shores of the Bosphorus!

CHAPTER XVI

MORE ABOUT HAREM LIFE ON THE
BOSPHORUS

THE house itself is built as most Turkish
houses are built, with two separate
entrances—the Haremlik and the Selamlik—
and a central entrance hall, arranged as a
lounge, from which all the other rooms can be
entered. The lounge on the ground floor is
marble tiled and in the centre is a fountain
which has long ceased to play. There are chairs
uncomfortably near the ground and unsteady-
looking coffee tables, and the whole place has
not yet recovered from the recent overflowing
of the Bosphorus, a substantial piece of the
front door being amongst other things missing.

The front door possesses neither knocker
nor bell. To obtain admission one kicks or
bangs, but not too violently, for the whole thing
would yield before very little pressure.

And the arrival at the house itself! How
strange! The springless old wagon which comes
to the boat to meet one, and the faded green
curtains which are discreetly pulled along a rusty

rod to hide us from the glances of the passers-by!
The weary old horse, not too securely roped to
the springless wagon, which rumbles and jaunts
over the "self-made" paths! The inhabitants
peeping through the latticed windows as we
rumble by! How and where we were going to
I just began to wonder, when the turban-headed
coachman drew up at the dilapidated, God-for-
saken-looking dwelling where I now am staying
But, really is "God-forsaken" the word to use?
"God-forsaken," when the Turks have a comfortable habit of leaving all the hard housework
to God Himself! He sends His rain to wash
the steps and clean the windows. His wind
blows away the dust. His sun kills the microbes
and dries the dampness. He makes the fruit
and flowers to come in their right season, and
the Turk looks on. . . .

Three or four kicks and several sharp umbrella-
taps at the door, and we obtain admission. The
male who opens for us first looks at me curiously
and then smiles, whilst Taqui, emerging from
behind a palm as big as a small tree, takes us
all in her arms, and welcomes me with such
vehemence that my hair comes tumbling down.
That means good luck, says she. That is
compensation!

A good, kind, sympathetic soul is Taqui. She
was given as wife to the gardener as a reward
for his years of faithful service, and had borne
him a substantial family, all of whom live on

the premises and walk in and out of the salons as they please, except when there are *visites de cérémonie.* I feel honoured to be classed as a member of the family ; and also *visites de cérémonie,* which are rare in Turkey, come quickly and leave quickly, whilst I have come to take up my residence for as long as it pleases me to stay. Taqui must have been born somewhere within the influence of the " Joconde," for she had the face and the wicked smile of the much-discussed Italian, or perhaps had the real " Joconde" Armenian ancestors ?

She is a hard worker, judging from Oriental standards, and used to complain bitterly about the lazy Turks, and as she takes her place at the head of the procession of slaves carrying beds she urges her companions to hurry, or the beds will never be made. Sometimes, however, even she forgets herself and pauses as she carries the mattresses to listen to some favourite song. At the end of the first verse she drops her mattress, sits on it during the second, and then, having given way so far, she waits until the singing is over. But it is not often that Taqui goes astray, and considering how many times she kept the others from committing this Turkish failing—killing time—a little margin should be allowed her from time to time.

There is a beautiful old woman in the household whom I long to " Kodak." Once I thought I " had " her as she sat cross-legged on the carpet rolling her quarter-hourly cigarette, but she noticed me, alas! then cursed, screamed, and buried her head in her roomy pantaloons. I shall not repeat the experiment.

This old lady is a personage in her way. Years before, she attempted to visit the Holy Tomb at Mecca, and although she never really got there, having lost all her worldly possessions in consequence, those kind friends who gave her shelter when she returned penniless always addressed her by the title " Hadgi," a title given to those pilgrims who go for their salvation to the Holy Tomb.

Hadgi loved the young master of the house more than the whole world. She was at his birth and at his mother's birth. Her great wish was to see the master's own little son make his appearance on life's scene. But the young master had acquired Western tastes, and in spite of the teachings of the Koran, in spite of all the privileges the Koran offers to those who enter into " holy matrimony," the young master was twenty-five, and had not yet taken unto himself a wife, nor was he thinking of doing so.

It was this question of the master's future that was tormenting poor old Hadgi when my visit began. She did not care for my appearance in a hat, but when I sat beside her on the floor and threaded her needle and tucked away inside my veil all my hair, the old woman's heart melted, and she

promptly offered me not only the master of the
house but all her worldly goods—four hand-woven
coarse chemises, exquisitely embroidered, which,
tied up in a handkerchief, remained beside her
on the floor all day; at night, still tied up in a
handkerchief, an honour paid by women to the
Koran, beside her bed.   To me, these chemises
were more like armour than *lingerie* and of not
the slightest use; they were, however, placed
beside my bed for two nights, then given back to
their owner, and she rejoiced more over the return
of her lost chemises than over any present I could
have made her.   Dear old Hadgi, she could be
such a sweet angel. She tied me up with charms to
protect me from the evil eye, she sang to me and
admired me and loved me, but only as long as I
was veiled.   When I wore a hat I was a stranger
to her—not one of the " faithful "; and when I
went to sit beside her, her usually benevolent
face clouded, her eyes flamed, and she rose from
the floor and hobbled away, casting at me a look
which being interpreted might have been, " What
are you doing beside me, Giaour? Whose religion
is the better—yours or mine? I shall see you
do no mischief here. . . ."

.   .   .   .   .

The kitchen is a hundred yards from the house
and the same distance from the dining-room.   It
is quite an independent building and a really
excellent idea for those who object to kitchen
" odours." There is to balance this convenience,

however, the fact that should it rain or snow the soup increases in quantity and the vegetables have water added to the oil, and oil and water do not mix, also Taqui is tempted on the way to question one of her children as to where he is going and what he is doing or likely to be doing; but still, to those who really do not know what is supposed to be hot and what cold, it does not matter.

The kitchen building is thick with ivy and creepers; even its unpoetic chimney is encircled with a wealth of roses which spread all around a welcome and delightful perfume. Above all, however, I love the garden. In the days that had been, it was planted and cared for and attached in terraces, as it were, to the side of a hill. Now it is left to the freedom of its own sweet will, and the roses, jasmin, carnations, lilies, and violets which grow all the year round are vying with one another for supremacy. Everywhere the roses have an easy victory, for it is they who can climb best, and they have climbed over every convenient inch of territory they can find. Exquisite, glorious roses they are! It seems a sin to pluck them in order to make jam, especially in a land where the women have a pathetic tenderness for flowers.

"You mustn't pluck a flower when the sun has gone to rest," they tell one, "for then the souls are coming into the flowers and you would kill a little soul about to be born." So I respect the little souls that are being born, and wander along the weed-grown paths, roses tearing my silk

dress, roses tearing my veil. Who could be unhappy in a garden when the sun has drawn out
all around a most perfect concert in perfumery—
roses, lilies, jasmin, carnations, and violets?
When I am back in my country I will see what
the distiller can make of this concert ; it will be
to me a souvenir of this beautiful garden of the
East where I have dreamt and where I was glad,
and at the same time sad ; where I have longed
and hoped and am resigned. How far are
the perfumes of " Araby " responsible for the
destinies of its curious people ?

"In my country," said I to my friends, "the
book of ' saws ' has it that those who love flowers
are born to sorrow." " No doubt, no doubt,"
they answer, "but we will bear with the sorrow,
for no Oriental can do without the flowers."

CHAPTER XVII

INCONSISTENCIES ON THE SHORES OF THE BOSPHORUS

I HAVE been to stay with Zeyneb at her little Yali on the shores of the Bosphorus. I had not seen her since she so resolutely and for ever closed the book of her European experiences, and our first meeting was just a little painful. Zeyneb is a dear friend—a curious, interesting study—a woman who had gone forth with a flourish of trumpets to try the great, wonderful liberty of the West,—a woman who cast aside her own civilization to throw herself before the altar of ours. She was not prepared for our civilization, she was not armed for the fray, the hurricane of progress took her off her feet, and now . . . she is back in the little Yali again.

This time I came in a caïque, for the house is right on the water's edge. It looked from the river like a tiny house—almost a Henley villa— yet once inside, it grew and grew, and every room seemed to give birth to a new one. I felt as though I were visiting a genealogical tree. . . .

I cannot master Turkish architecture—at least, this funny place has entirely upset my calculations. Perhaps in the days when polygamy was practised the master of the house, beginning with one wife, built the façade, then extended his premises as he extended his family; the fact that his eighth wife is still living permits me to make this bold supposition. A hateful idea it is, to have rooms with more than one door; it's like having people with eyes in the back of their heads, and I wonder whether there is not also a door under my bed and one in the ceiling. It's rather uncanny too, for in a country where doors have no locks and would not lock if they had, every one flits unheard into one another's room. . . .

Fortunately there is some one in all the three rooms leading out of mine. I have a big brass bed with mother-of-pearl decorations, the mattress is comfortable, so surely, being very tired, I will sleep. I close my eyes, and shortly afterwards wake with a start. In the semi-darkness I see a figure in my room; I call out in some language. "Don't be afraid," replies the figure, "it is Zeyneb." She has been to fetch a fire lest I should be cold. In her one hand is the brass *mongal*, about the size of a pail, which throws out a welcome heat, and in the other a big silver tea-pot to warm the water for my bottle after I am sound asleep. "Don't be afraid," again says my hostess, but it is just a little strange to see in the dim moonlight a long, sweeping dressing-gown, a turban-headed figure armed with a *mongal* and a teapot.

As time goes on, however, I grow accustomed to these nocturnal invasions and too lazy even to acknowledge them. Sometimes it is my left neighbour who comes in to help herself to my candies or my syrup, sometimes my back neighbour wonders, since she cannot sleep, whether I am also awake, and if so perhaps a story . . ., and sometimes Zeyneb wakes me to see whether I am dead, so peacefully do I sleep.

I am invited to coffee in the Selamlik. Zeyneb must not accompany me, she who was a Western club woman—she who ate *décolletée* in the presence of men. . . .

A charming diplomatist who is there—he is a Turk of the old school—rises politely when I enter and asks permission to talk for a few moments to his brother diplomatist, a European, in French. Their conversation is charming and interesting—both speak French with a curious, original construction. What kind of French construction shall I have acquired, I wonder, by the time I return to Paris?

But the Turk has me on his conscience—he cuts his conversation down to the lowest possible brevity, and then *en galant homme* comes right down to my level!

I asked him for political news. " Mademoiselle is very polite," said he ; but he would not allow me to sacrifice myself in that manner. I remained firm, so did he. "Poetry for women," said he, "politics for men." "In my country women like politics better than poetry," said I. "Yes," he answered, "but not you. I have seen pictures of your political women!"

We were to go for a picnic—a mysterious little semi-Western performance, and no one was to know about it. Our plan of action was soon determined.

It is noon and we have already lunched. A springless wagon is before the door. Thickly veiled, we get in and the curtains are drawn. A short while after another wagon starts. This wagon will follow us, but it does not convey veiled women. Let me at once confess, it contains as many men as we are women. What a bold adventure!

The men are Turkish gentlemen, and will keep within the confidence of our little circle what we are rash enough to do. There is amongst our party *une jeune fille à marier*, and we would not care to wreck her matrimonial prospects for any pleasure, great or small, that might be ours. . . .

A charming drive it is—a little long perhaps, but the jolting of the carriage is exercise in Turkey. One has every horseback sensation from walking to jibbing, except a good canter.

Along the zig-zag path we plunge. We catch hold of one another as we dive into the holes;

we crawl up the hills and crawl down, and finally arrive at the forest and at the lake where we are to meet.

It is a sleepy, beautiful lake covered with pink and white water-lilies, and a little old boat has been taken prisoner amongst them.

Not long after our arrival we are joined by the Selamlik. I don't know any of the men, and we are introduced and bow in the picturesque fashion, carefully keeping our hair covered, and we speak to them as naturally as though we were in the West.

Together we admire the beautiful nature around. We speak of the war—we speak of the future—we make plans for Turkey, and the men present us each with boxes of cigarettes and chocolates, and eat them with us until the sinking sun reminds us that it is time for us to be returning the way we came. Then the two sexes—the Harem and the Selamlik—are separated again, but both feel better for the little interlude.

We have done no harm, nor is our adventure particularly thrilling, though charming all the same. Perhaps after all the Turks are right— they can give to innocence, as we cannot, a lovely dash of wickedness.

.   .   .   .   .

One more household to stay with and my visits on the shores of the Bosphorus must be ended. Fâtima wants me back, and that is sufficient

excuse for my leaving my friends without offending them. Also, it is getting very chilly near
the Bosphorus, and already the general exodus
back to Constantinople has begun.

I watch the removal carts packed with luggage
passing before the windows. Sometimes it is a
donkey or a series of donkeys who remove the
goods on their backs, but whether it be cart
or donkey the things have a peculiar habit of
falling off or out, and but for an honest passer-by
who draws the driver's attention to the fallen
articles, they would be lost. And all this takes
time, and yet the Turk says, " Why hurry ? One's
destination will not walk away." . . .

I am now to stay with the family of a Cherif
—a high dignitary of the Moslem church. In
this family the division between Harem and
Selamlik is strictly kept—and such a family
will be the last to cast aside any of the traditions
or superstitions that have crept in like a weed
to spoil and strangle Islam.

.   .   .   .   .

My visit is over. It has been interesting as
an experience, but not one man have we seen
for one week, for as the Cherif may see no
woman farther removed in blood than a sister
—and there are generally other women visitors
there—he cannot come to the harem.

In this household, only one lady spoke French,
and that not at all well ; added to this, she is
timid and prefers rather not to speak than to

give me an opportunity of criticising her. Our conversation therefore is reduced to signs, and our pleasures to eating and drinking. We have the east side of the house, the men the west; and we each have a separate garden, and a wall that no one would dare to climb separates us.

Our long unending meals are still longer since I require both my hands to talk with. An old negress insists on filling up my plate with good things. "I simply can't," I say to her in English; she laughs the bereks off the dish. Then she explains to me with signs which the French speaker finally puts into French: "*Beaucoup corps, beaucoup manger.*"

In the afternoons, since we cannot speak, we try on all kinds of costumes and drink coffee, the ladies always taking possession of my grounds to see whether something good is not in store for me. A sign of "abundance" is always there, but since the interpreter has never been able to define the kind of abundance to which I am limited, let us hope an abundance of all kinds of good things is coming.

It is a curious household and quite without interest to me after one day. A weary round of days exactly the same—women who know little of their own land and nothing of any other. I begin to feel myself a "sin" in such surroundings. Perhaps after my visit these women will begin to think. They were

13

perfectly happy before I came; will they still be happy after I have left? Yes, I believe so. Some power has arranged their life as it is. Were that power to wish it otherwise, that power would change it. Every nation must have doormats at its threshold.

CHAPTER XVIII

ONLOOKERS ONLY

AND now the time has come for me to return to my native land, I ask myself what have been my final impressions of my life as a Turkish woman. All these weeks, which have slipped by without my noticing their going, I have felt like an actress seated in the theatre, watching another play my part—indeed a restful sensation.

I came here with perhaps just a little of the "downtrodden woman of the East" fallacy left, but that has now completely vanished. To me, an Englishwoman, there are sides of this life which would irritate me into open rebellion. That the customs of the country should have power to make me wear a veil, whether I wished it or not, that I should be forced to travel in a compartment reserved exclusively for women, that I must always have the hood up when I drive in a carriage, that if I chance to stray into a café of the people, I am served in a superior kind of rabbit-hutch, separated by a grating from the opposite sex, that if I go into a tea-shop where there are men, I will be

requested to leave, and last, but not least, that
I should have to depend for male society exclusively on my blood relations—Heaven indeed
forbid!

A Turkish woman asked me once what it felt
like to be able to mix freely with men who are
not blood relations. " I cannot *tell*," I answered;
" it dates right back to the time when my big
brother teased me to tears, and his friend wiped
them away. To ask me what it means to mix
freely with men is almost like asking what it
means to have lungs. I never stopped to think,
but I know I should die without them."

But then, after all, is not everything relative?
Had I never known the pleasures of male
society, had not circumstances forced me to
take my life in my own hands and work out
my own destiny, I should not perhaps quarrel
with what is part of a Turkish woman's existence.
If we in the West possess what is known as
the "joy of liberty," have not so many of us
been denied the blessing of protection? The
veiled Turkish woman asks, Can you imagine
how distressing it is to be willing to work and
for the conventions of the country not to allow
it? Many of the poor tired workers of my
country might ask, Can you imagine what it is
to have to work and not to be able to find work?

All these weeks I have been leading a Turkish
existence. I have really tried to put myself in
a Turkish woman's place, but I cannot somehow

pity her. Is it that I have been too near the
suffering heart of my own countrywomen ? "Our
lives are so empty," pointed out one woman.
" Really we do not have enough social dis-
tractions." I close my eyes and think of the
women of my own country, worn out with a
London season and its festivities. In their
moments of sincerity they would not tell you
they had expended their time and energy only
to be bored ; but social obligations cannot be
taken in moderate doses, you must swallow the
whole draught.

" Can you imagine what it is to have longed
all your life to hear Wagner and a full orchestra
and not to be able ? " said one woman ; and
another, who is an exceedingly good musician, tells
me she has no idea of her own value as a pianist,
seeing she never had an opportunity of hearing
professionals.

But all this is changing, and it is a passionately
interesting study to see them taking off the
customs of ages to put on something different.
How will they appear when next I visit them ?

I have called the Turkish woman an "on-
looker." She is at present, as it were, only on
the margin of the great life ; she understands
enough of the game, however, to long to take
a part. How will she play that part ? Is it
absolutely necessary for her to come to us for
assistance ?

This is the question I have asked so many

Turkish women. They must think I argue almost like a reactionary. Yet I have not defended the harem system. There is, however, so much in the Turkish home life which is beautiful that I would prefer to see them progressing on the lines of their own civilization, rather than becoming a poor imitation of us. Let them come to us and learn to organize their studies; the rest they can, if they will, manage for themselves.

But I have a feeling that, except for a very few, Turkish women will not take too kindly to our civilization. When my charming English friends, who reconcile me just a little to Pera, took me to the Dorcas Ball I felt uncomfortable prickings of conscience, going to enjoy myself and leaving my friends at home. I might have saved my regrets, however, for it was they who were sorry for me, having to waste my time dancing till the small hours of the morning with mere acquaintances.

And those Turkish women who have come to Europe? How well they have adapted themselves to our civilization. When they were with us who could have supposed they were wearing hats for the first time? Who could suppose, to hear them speaking our language, to see them threading their way in and out of the traffic of our big capitals, that they had not lived with us all their lives? And yet how glad they were to return to their own home life!

The Turk has always been most severely
attacked in Europe on the manner in which he
treats his womenkind. He considers them, it is
said, " mere possessions." But surely this is the
case with the men of most nations. On what
but this is the woman's rebellion based?

That the Moslem woman has no status, I most
emphatically deny. If the Moslem women are
" possessions," they are " cherished possessions "
and treated as such. Are Moslem women obliged
to exercise the most hideous of professions as are
their Christian neighbours? Is there anywhere
in the East the terrible degradation of our poor
Whitechapel women? It is not because he
despises her that the Turk has kept his woman-
kind screened from the world. Her rôle is
maternity, therefore the cares and temptations of
the world must not be known to her, and nothing
ought to interfere with this supreme reason of
her existence.

Quite recently a decision of the greatest importance and daring was taken by the Ottoman
Government. Without their having to ask, the
University was thrown open to women, and they
are now attending lectures on gynæcology,
hygiene, woman's rights, etc.

When I heard the news, much as I rejoiced,
I could not help making a comparison between
the methods of the East and those of the West.
Here are these "unspeakable" Turks giving to
women privileges for which they have not asked,

simply because they are theirs by right, and
since they are to take their place as workers in
the world, they must be educated. And yet,
here in England, much as women have tried to
work along the lines of evolution they have been
driven to revolution. Is this sex antagonism of
their asking? From the beginning of the
woman's movement, every privilege has had to
be bought with rebellion.

.   .   .   .   .

And now, with reluctance, I close the diary of
my existence as a Turkish woman. I have not
attempted to give a careful and finished picture
of my life here ; this is the age of impressions,
and the beautiful Eastern colouring would lose
much of its warmth, were it not put on fresh from
the brush. My boxes are corded and ready, the
Messageries Maritimes steamer which brought me
here will take me back through the beautiful Sea
of Marmora, where the setting sun casts itself in
such magnificence on to the water beneath it,
and the dolphins bathed in sunlight pop up to
greet us as we pass along.

A little Turkish friend is going to Europe
with me. Her first hat is in readiness, and when
the steamer has gone through the " Dardanelles "
she will put it on.

If only I could order the same calm sea which
brought me here to take me back again ; but I
must trust to Providence. All through my visit
the glorious sun of Eastern hospitality has been

darting its beams upon me—it has been a wonderful experience.

Ah! the beautiful unceremoniousness of the East, the absolute sincerity, the liking of one's friends for friendship's sake irrespective of position, and the true brotherhood and democracy of the kindly Turk . . . if these qualities must vanish in the inevitable march of progress, then may I never see Turkey again ; for, without these qualities, it would no longer be the Turkey I have admired and loved.

AFTER-WORDS

IT was Christmas 1913. The Balkan War was over, and Young Turkey had begun with a patriotism born of humiliation to save what remained of the poor mutilated Father-land. (I have described my impressions of Turkish life during this period.)

At the head of affairs were men who could accept responsibility. Seeds of progress were being sown amongst the ruins. The leaders, who had learnt their lesson from bitter ex-perience and had accomplished so much against terrible odds, could they not now steer the ship of State into the calm waters of prosperity?

Talaat-Djavid and Djémal knew what they wanted. Though confronted with international and internal problems, difficulties of race and religion and financial chaos, yet they kept their heads, and then they made one fatal mistake—that mistake was ENVER PASHA.

Only a year ago Enver was neither Pasha nor the Sultan's son-in-law nor Minister of War. He was lying seriously ill at the German hospital

at Constantinople, and only his great determination to serve his country pulled him successfully
through three terrible operations. He had been
fighting in spite of appendicitis, and in spite of all
kinds of internal complications and bullet wounds.
He was brought almost dead from the battlefield—
even German surgery had given him up—and yet he
would not die. Enver struck one as a picturesque
personage. His energy and determination were
such new features in Turkish civilization. A
fearless and reckless soldier, tall, handsome, a
patriot certainly, unintelligent but sincere, hated
and loved in so many harems, his picture was
to be found draped in the Turkish flag : he was
the best selling of picture postcards.

Accompanied by Enver's great friend and
master, Djémal Pasha, I went to visit the Turkish
hero in the German hospital. It was then I
discovered what Djémal afterwards owned was
true, that Enver was totally lacking in initiative
and imagination, and that he could only command
when he himself was commanded, but no one
better than he could obey. " And the revolution
of 1908 ? " I asked. " How splendidly he carried
out his orders ! " I was told. " He's a magnificent
fellow, and such a man is *indispensable* to our
cause."

Although weak, Enver discussed many political
questions with us, but in everything he agreed
with his friend Djémal Pasha, whose sympathies
were entirely Franco-British, because, as he ex-

plained, and rightly so, Britain and France were
the two countries who had no interest to work
for Turkey's destruction. Djémal detested
Germany even more than he detested Russia.
He loved England, but more than England
he loved France and everything French, and
French culture and thought, and he once added,
" *French money*." Djémal's policy was to allow
Turkey to be under the greatest obligations to
England and France. If only England and
France would come forward and do this and that
for us, if France would offer us education, if
England, as the ruler of our co-religionists, would
come nearer to us, where then would be German
influence?

The German Mission had just then arrived
in Constantinople. My Turkish women friends
were much distressed, considering it a humiliation
to see their capital thus invaded by Teutons.
Indeed, they requested me, in their name, to
ask the Government whether the Mission could
not be removed to Adrianople. Djémal could
not understand the women's anxiety about
Germany. "We have begun with German
methods and we must go on," said he; "but the
German mission has no political meaning. . . ."
Djémal was always sincere. His god was power.
He wanted power above everything.

And so Enver, as a useful *instrument* of his
colleagues, and particularly Djémal, was appointed
Minister of War. As their obedient servant in

his own reckless manner, he was to obey their orders; he was to sweep out from the War Office old worn-out servants; to make other drastic changes his friends found indispensable; but his rôle was distinctly to obey, not to command. He fulfilled his mission; he *did* obey, but he changed masters—he gave himself up body and soul, not to his colleagues, but to the German Kaiser.

When Enver so emphatically denied to me the Germanophilism of which he was accused, no doubt he was sincere. He was like a man in love. He, as a soldier of an army suffering from lack of discipline, could not help admiring the German organisation. Their arrogance also appealed to him, and although, as a democrat and a man of the people, he tried to persuade himself to the contrary, he was flattered by the Emperor William's attention. In Berlin, when military attaché, they, the Germans, made a god of Enver; he left his heart in Germany, too, it is said. He may have tried to escape from this German influence; he simply could not: it was his destiny. He who loved to obey found his master at Potsdam and his master's representatives at Constantinople—the Ambassador, Baron von Wangenheim, and General Liman von Sanders, head of the German Mission. They took possession of him; he was powerless; as powerless as his ex-master, Djémal, to take a firm stand once more for Franco-British influence.

It was Christmas Eve a year ago. The

Turkish heir to the throne invited me *tout à fait sans cérémonie* to his palace to coffee and to talk to him about my country. Although he could perfectly understand French, he could not speak it ; consequently Djémal Pasha was good enough to act as interpreter.

The Prince's knowledge of everything connected with my country was a pleasant surprise. He admired and loved England. "Whatever political mistakes we may say England has made, however unjustly we may think she has treated us," said the Prince, " England is still our model. She's a clean, honour-loving nation, a nation of gentlemen." These sentiments were shared by the Grand Vizier.

The Prince was not as enthusiastic about France as Djémal Pasha. France to him meant Paris, and Paris was a danger to Young Turkey. " Let our men go to France afterwards, but let them first be sobered down in England," said he. " French learning may be fine, but England gives a young man character. . . . English women make their sons men. We want Turks to be men." To our statesmen the Prince paid tribute ; also to our Court, our literature, and our architecture. " It is all aristocratic and solid," were his words. . . .

The Turkish heir to the throne considered German influence something that did not even come within the range of discussion. "Germany," said he, " is forty years old ; she has yet to be tried." Then he added, " Britain has shed her blood for us—that we can never forget."

Such is the opinion of the future Sultan of Turkey about Britain—now Turkey's enemy—and indeed, he meant every word he said.

And in the harems—does Germany even count? Right in the heart of Asia Minor, they have heard of British honour, but who has heard of Germany? and the name of Britain rests on a prestige which has stood the test of time. That "*all right*" verdict which was given to the English governess—that acceptance of the British word without contract—are facts which count.

An ill-advised Government can lead its country to destruction, but the mighty Kaiser himself cannot crush out this admiration born in the Turks for England.

It is true England and France have never considered Turkey worth while, as Germany has done. I said so to a British official. " We cannot send out retrievers, as Baron Marschall does," he answered. " We can only offer a straightforward friendship. If the Turks cannot accept that . . ."

Yet Germany did send her finest diplomatists to Constantinople, and also her picked officers ; the Kaiser himself paid court to the Sultan, and on his Eastern tour saw that Moslem feelings and customs were in every way considered. He gave presents of great value to

both the Sultan and his Grand Vizier. Kiamil
Pasha in his Konak has books of priceless
value given to him by the Kaiser, and yet
evidently it was of little value, for the veteran
statesman of Turkey turned always to England
for sympathy.   England was the country who
could put everything right, and one of his
greatest sorrows was that England had not
come to Turkey's assistance in her hour of
need.

And Turkey's quarrel in this case was
certainly not with Britain. She was still smart-
ing under what she felt the injustice of giving
Mitylene and Chios to Greece.   Day and
night she was waiting for an opportunity to
get back her islands, and day and night she
was in terror lest Greece should strike before
her Dreadnoughts—ordered in England—were
ready. Hakky Pasha, the ex-Grand Vizier of
Turkey in London, telegraphed and advised
that in spite of Germany's offer of assistance
against Greece, Turkey must remain neutral,
and to attack Greece even during the present
war classed her at once as anti-British. But
it was not what any reasonable statesman
wanted, it was what Germany wanted.   Turkey
was clamouring for war with Greece; instead of
this she found that Germany in her name had
bombarded an open Russian port!   Germany
promised her Mitylene and Chios and even
Cyprus.   She staked her whole fortune on

German victory and German honour—and
Germany promised to free her from European
interference. Now, it is not difficult to
calculate what Turkey has gained from the
speculation.

It is hard to make out a good case for
Turkey, but however bitter one may feel against
the foolish Enver and the Young Turkish
Government, the Turkish people are not to
blame. A friend writing from Turkey tells
me Germany left no stone unturned to lead
the Government into difficulties. In Anatolia,
she spread the false report that the Moslems
in the Caucasus were being ill treated by the
Russians! Baron von Wangenheim took possession of the press. Enver Pasha, led by Baron
von Wangenheim, made short work of those
who under the eyes of their new masters
declared they had put up too long with this
"mad Government." Djémal Pasha's orders
that the *Goeben* and *Breslau* should be disarmed
were totally disregarded; the German Admiral
Suchon was master of the situation, and
refused to take on board the Turkish sailors
sent by Djémal. Turkey ceased to exist.

The rest of the story is known: the touching
"Good-bye" which passed between the British
and French Ambassadors and the Grand Vizier,
the arrival of three million marks which was
Germany's first instalment of a river of gold
she had promised to her faithful Enver. Then

14

a time of waiting and the second instalment of gold—German paper!!! Turkey is now quite aware of the treachery of Germany. But it is too late.

"There is no happiness and no salvation for the Turk," a dear friend writes me. "However much we try, whatever sacrifices we make, our lot has always been, and always will be, to be sacrificed to the ambitions of the European Powers. Once more Turkey has fulfilled her destiny. . . ."

.　　　.　　　.　　　.　　　.

It was Christmas only a year ago. The land of Islam was wrapped in a mantle of snow. To the quiet harem came Turkish friends from far and near, and together we celebrated the birth of the Saviour of the World. It was a beautifully pathetic Christmas, one of the most interesting and wonderful I ever spent.

The celebration of Christmas in a Moslem home! As a little girl, I longed and dreamed of the day when I should be privileged to tell the Moslems the great and real meaning of Christmas. . . . And that day had come.

We had a Christmas tree, we played at snapdragon and hunt the slipper and musical chairs. We sang "Auld lang syne," and to me it was the beginning of a great understanding—a great wide brotherhood—and we promised to spend this Christmas together in the same real Christmas manner. . . .

And that was Christmas a year ago. Could I ever have dreamed where I would be this year? I, who had a year ago explained the beautiful real meaning of Christmas, am here in a French hospital with English nurses helping to repair the ills that Christian nations have done to one another!

What a glorious example for the Moslem peoples! The hideousness of the Christian's warfare! Is there anything the East can now learn from the West?

There are Christmas trees in all the hospital wards. The English nurses have dressed them . . . the bare walls are transformed into a fairyland of ivy and candles and real good Christmas decorations. There are cakes and sweets and fruits and British plum pudding. . . .

Luncheon has ended. These splendid English nurses, who have responded to the French appeal to come and help, ask me for a toast.

"There is only one toast for all thinking humanity," I reply, and the nurses understand.

The German prisoners are washing up the dishes on which we have eaten our British plum pudding. Poor pathetic souls! Let us distinguish between the criminal and his crime. . . .

And this is the Christmas I promised to spend in Turkey—the land where I have spent so many happy days of my life. And this is the result of the world-famed Teuton *Kultur*

Beside the crimes of Louvain and Rheims and the poor shivering and hungry refugees who were first wrecked at Havre and then brought on penniless and homeless here to Bordeaux, and all the other crimes for which Germany must answer, I place the betrayal of Turkey. To deliberately lead to destruction a people who made so brave a stand for regeneration, whose patriotism I have so inadequately described, if this is all that civilization can produce—if this is how we illustrate the lessons we have learnt from Bethlehem to Gethsemane—how can we any longer preach that wonderful gospel of peace and goodwill amongst men?

My companions urge this is the darkness before dawn. Behind the clouds and battle smoke the sun is shining. Cruel platitudes in a hospital of eleven hundred wounded soldiers. And when the war is over? Alas, the unending sadness of my surroundings has killed for a while any hope of happiness.

HOSPITAL MILITAIRE DE TALENCE,
BORDEAUX, *Christmas* 1914.

INDEX